A REMARKABLE FESTIVAL

A REMARKABLE FESTIVAL

Photographs from the Fiftieth Wexford Festival
by PÁDRAIG GRANT

Introduction by COLM TÓIBÍN

Festival history by IAN FOX

Published in 2002 by Wexford Festival Opera.

All rights reserved. No part of this publication may be reproduced, stored in a retrieval system or transmitted in any form or by any means, electronic, mechanical, photocopying, recording or otherwise, without the prior permission of the publishers.

Photographs by Pádraig Grant.
Photographs on pages 46, 55, 56, 57, 58, 59, 71, 80, 82, 83 & 87 by Anna Papaconstantinou.

Production photographs and illustrations courtesy of Derek Speirs (pages 112, 116, 117, 118), Amelia Stein (pages 107, 108, 110) and the Wexford Festival Opera Archive.

Book designed by John Foley at Bite,
Grand Parade, Cork, Ireland. Telephone 021 4275988
www.bitedesign.com

ISBN: 0-9543527-0-X
ISBN: 0-9543527-1-8 (pbk.)

Wexford Festival Opera
Theatre Royal
High Street
Wexford
Ireland

www.wexfordopera.com

10 9 8 7 6 5 4 3 2 1

the arts council
schomhairle
ealaíon

Wexford Festival Opera is grant aided by The Arts Council

DIAGEO
IRELAND

The Festival appreciates the support for this publication of its principal sponsor Guinness (a Diageo company)

Contents

1. *A Strange Beauty* by Colm Tóibín — 7

2. *A Remarkable Festival* by Pádraig Grant — 11

3. *A Spirit of Confidence* by Ian Fox — 91

4. Artists & repertoire at Wexford Festival 1951 - 2001 — 119

5. Index of artists at Wexford Festival 1951 - 2001 — 150

A Strange Beauty

BY COLM TÓIBÍN

The town itself has a strange beauty in the washed light of the early winter. It is not hard to imagine that boats once sailed from here to Buenos Aires, that in the early years of the last century the long quays of Wexford were busy with trade and traffic. That is all faded now; the harbour has silted up. But the town still looks like a medieval port town, and the atmosphere of Wexford is full of the rich mixtures which the harbour and the fertile hinterland combined to make. The town got its name from the Vikings, and clearly remained an important centre of trade, but its tone was set by the Normans. Half the names of the people are Norman, and in the plainness of the architecture, and the lack of pretension in the citizens, there is a Norman austerity. The other elements include not only the Gaelic, but also the English and Hugenot.

Thus the two famous writers from the town - John Banville and Billy Roche - have surnames which are Hugenot and Norman but backgrounds which are mixed. Roche's work is full of the sadness of the town; history for him has enough associations in just one generation. He has a way of placing a halo around ordinary speech, finding a common phrase and making it sound like a poetic moment of truth. Banville's Wexford, which appears sporadically in his work, could be a light-filled town on the sea anywhere in the Northern hemisphere. In Banville's novel 'Mephisto', Wexford could be a Hanseatic town. Banville is concerned to clarify and illuminate and make more mysterious the central matters of order and chaos, memory and imagination, language truth and logic. Roche presents a Wexford full of talk, he is interested in spiritual topography; on the other hand, Banville's tone is much grander. Yet both of them are part of that cultural diversity that makes Wexford different.

For Roche, there is no one ordinary in the town; just as ordinary speech can be rendered poetic, so too ordinary lives can be filled with drama, can be made memorable. Banville's work is proof that anything can happen; his genius as a phrase-maker and his tone, Modernist and ironic, can, almost despite itself, produce work that is deeply affecting. If anything can explain why the Opera Festival has thrived in Wexford and why it is so fundamental to the fabric of the town, it is this business of Wexford being special enough, and rich and diverse enough, to produce two such writers, whose talents seem to pull in opposite directions.

· · ·

The train journey along the river Slaney between Enniscorthy and Wexford remains for me the most moving and resonant landscape anywhere in the world. In that silvery still afternoon light, for several miles you see no roads and hardly any buildings, just trees and the calm strong river. If you are travelling to Wexford in late October, with the promise of music, these ten or fifteen minutes offer a special happiness.

All of us have a landscape of the soul, places whose contours and resonances are etched into us and haunt us. If we ever became ghosts, these are the places to which we would return. There is a small single-lane bridge along that stretch of the Slaney called Macmine Bridge; it spans the river at its loneliest and most mysterious. If you stop for one second and look north, you can see the spire of Pugin's Cathedral at Enniscorthy rising over the other buildings of the town and the brown-green water below you cutting deep into the sandy soil, moving slowly towards Wexford and the sea.

Every time I stop here, I watch Macmine Bridge's own modest beauty stretching there between the two towns, and carrying with it, like the water below, a weight of memory and sadness. The depth of the November colours, the strong, sleeping textures of this landscape, the brooding dullness of the sky, the heavy water, all are beautiful now. I can remember everything here; this is a place where images come back one after the other, like a strange, random, vivid slide show.

It is 1971 in Wexford, for example, and I am sixteen. Those of us who want to go to the dress rehearsal of the opera have to assemble every afternoon before study to listen to the records and have the story explained. I have a clear memory of the stereo record player being rigged up and the light from the sea shining through the long windows of the school and the old broken down desks and the chipped wood of the wainscotting and the peeled paint. I have no memory of the music, however. Not a note from those afternoons has lingered in my memory, not a sound. And nothing of the story. And yet I know that I went there every afternoon for a week.

When my family came to visit, I casually mentioned what we were doing and I told them the name of the opera, 'The Pearl Fishers' by Bizet. My mother said that it had the most beautiful love duet in all opera and she tried to hum it, and she told the story of how two men, a tenor and a baritone, were in love with the same woman, and they managed the most beautiful love song in her honour. At home, she said, we had a record of John McCormack singing it. I can still see the record sleeve, blue and gold, and I know that later I listened to it. I think it was called 'The Golden Voice of John McCormack'. At the time of the opera, however, I had never paid any attention to it, being too wrapped up in James Taylor, Simon and Garfunkel and Leonard Cohen.

I know that I was in the upstairs gallery of the Theatre Royal during the dress rehearsal of the opera, but I could not have been very far back, because the lighting and the opening scene are clear in my mind, and seem close, and the extraordinary passion and precision of the singing are still with me. I know that the soprano was called Christiane Eda Pierre, but I have no idea of the names of the other soloists. Now, as I write this, the word 'motif' comes back to me. In the talks about the opera each afternoon, we were told to watch for motifs, but that did not sink in then as very important. Now, as I sat in the Theatre Royal, I recognised the motif which came before the first duet, but I was not ready for the live duet which came a great and beautiful shock - those soaring moments when the two voices merged and moved apart and competed and merged again. I wonder now if this was not only the beginning of my life as a follower of music, but of something much more central, if this was not the beginning of my conscious watching of things, already nostalgic for them, even before they had ended, trying to drink them in so that their emotional contours would never be forgotten.

It was difficult to forget that opera. If I had to place this in a novel now, I would have no difficulty writing the scene exactly as it was: standing outside the theatre that night, with the story of love and treachery in my head, and the soaring music and the suffering heroine and the dead hero fresh in my imagination, I felt that I was ready for anything except returning to the school and the dormitory and class in the morning. The dream had to fade, but it was the dream which remained real and fresh and memorable and inspiring. Most of our ordinary lives is forgotten; this night was extraordinary.

This is, I suppose, the legacy of opera in the nineteenth century: the idea that pure, raw emotion could be conjured up on the stage, unembarrassed and lacking all irony, and could be conveyed to us directly and clearly so that if you were ready for it, if you were young enough, or open enough, it would not merely entertain you, or amuse you, but it would change you.

• • •

Ten years later, I became a regular. I still cannot disassociate the music from the harbour itself and the light in Wexford and the memory of those teenage years in the town. I remember the first year when I had come back and I stayed at the Ferrycarrig Hotel and watched the dusk falling on what had been a clear blue day. There was a strange pink glow in the sky and a rosy edge to the light. For twenty minutes maybe Wexford estuary was still, there was no wind, a few seabirds moved, but not much else. And I already felt a longing for home, or for transcendence, or for something nameless and beyond myself.

And there still is nothing like that small theatre and its small audience settling down and waiting for the first notes of what will be a new adventure.

And I know that we should pay homage to those who managed this festival with such care and zeal and close attention to its core values - music and excellence. What is extraordinary about the opera festival at Wexford is how much has changed, but how much the sacred core has been preserved. The festival is longer; the opera house is bigger; the audience includes more Irish people, or seems to. But there is something wonderful and sacred about walking those streets in your best clothes on those early winter nights, when you know that you are going to see an opera you will probably never see again, an opera which has failed the test of time or perhaps deserves to be better known, or has strange flaws or hidden forgotten treasures.

In Ireland there is not much continuity. Because of poverty and general social deprivation, hardly anyone has inherited furniture, for example, and there are no festivals, with the exception of Christmas, which we have inherited from the nineteenth century, and we can hardly talk with much credibility about traditional Irish food. Thus the Wexford Festival has come to stand for endurance and continuity as well as excellence. It holds a peculiar position in national and local life; it is not a popular festival, as say the Fleadh Ceoil or the Rose of Tralee, and yet it commands enormous respect. It has been responsible, through the recitals, for the musical education of many thousands, and has also offered many others some of the musical highlights of their lives, some of the richest and most valuable cultural experiences they have ever had.

It is important to remember that it did not happen in Wexford by accident. The hidden poetic spirit of the town in the work of Billy Roche and the soaring spirit in the work of John Banville combined to make the festival's organisers both practical and inspirational. This was the same spirit which read the pamphlets about liberty in the 1790s and studied the example of the French Revolution and the American Revolution. This was the same spirit which brought Pugin, the greatest church architect of the age, to Wexford to design the cathedral at Enniscorthy, the chapel of St Peter's College and churches all over the county. This spirit means that any changes in the future will be carefully considered and implemented with flair and good judgement, but the festival will aim as it always has to allow that moment of pure madness or pure joy or pure magic or pure beauty on the stage greater scope, larger possibilities, sharper resonances. The success of the festival, its keenness for excellence, its sense of continuity and tradition make it an essential and exemplary aspect of contemporary Irish life.

Colm Tóibín is a native of Enniscorthy Co. Wexford and his novels include The South, The Heather Blazing *and* The Blackwater Lightship *which was nominated for The Booker Prize in 1999. He has been attending Wexford Festival since 1971.*

HIGH STREET The existence of a theatre on this High Street is always a surprise to the first time attendee. It runs along behind numbers 17 to 31 High Street. Numbers 19 and 21 have long been the foyer with number 17 added in the 1960's to become the Box Office. In more recent years the festival has purchased numbers 27 (1987), 21 (1992), 25 (1994), 23 (1999) and 33 (2002) and these are used as offices, foyer spaces, bars, props stores and cloakroom. In the impending development it is intended to maintain the unique streetscape.

LOOKING DOWN MARY STREET From this approach – still two way traffic! – one sees number 31 High Street. The upper floors were removed and the house now acts as storage for sets for the two productions not on stage at any give time.

FESTIVAL LOUNGE THEATRE ROYAL Repetiteurs and Stage Managers attend the Arrivals Reception for artists in the foyer of the Theatre Royal. Each year on a single day over one hundred people arrive through Dublin Airport and are transported to Wexford, check in to their accommodation – private houses, Bed and Breakfasts and apartments throughout the town and surrounding area – and arrive at the Theatre Royal for a welcoming reception. At 10am on the following morning, rehearsals begin.

THE FOUNDERS ROOM, THEATRE ROYAL Artists in rehearsal for *Sapho*

THEATRE ROYAL Production Manager David Stuttard making some notes following a rehearsal of *Sapho* at Theatre Royal. David lives in Belfast and has been Production Manager at the Festival since 1999.

Right: **THE POST ROOM AT 27 HIGH STREET** The "Post Room" generally commandeered by Stage Managers at the Festival becomes a hive of activity for seven weeks and on occasion debates are conducted on the notice board!

ST MICHAEL'S HALL Stage Manager Ann Brodie feigns shyness whilst working on *Jakobín*

Above & following pages **BARRACKS, BARRACK STREET** Ekatrina Morozova and Director Thomas de Mallet Burgess discuss a scene in *Alessandro Stradella* whilst Russian Repetiteur Ljuba Orfenova waits.

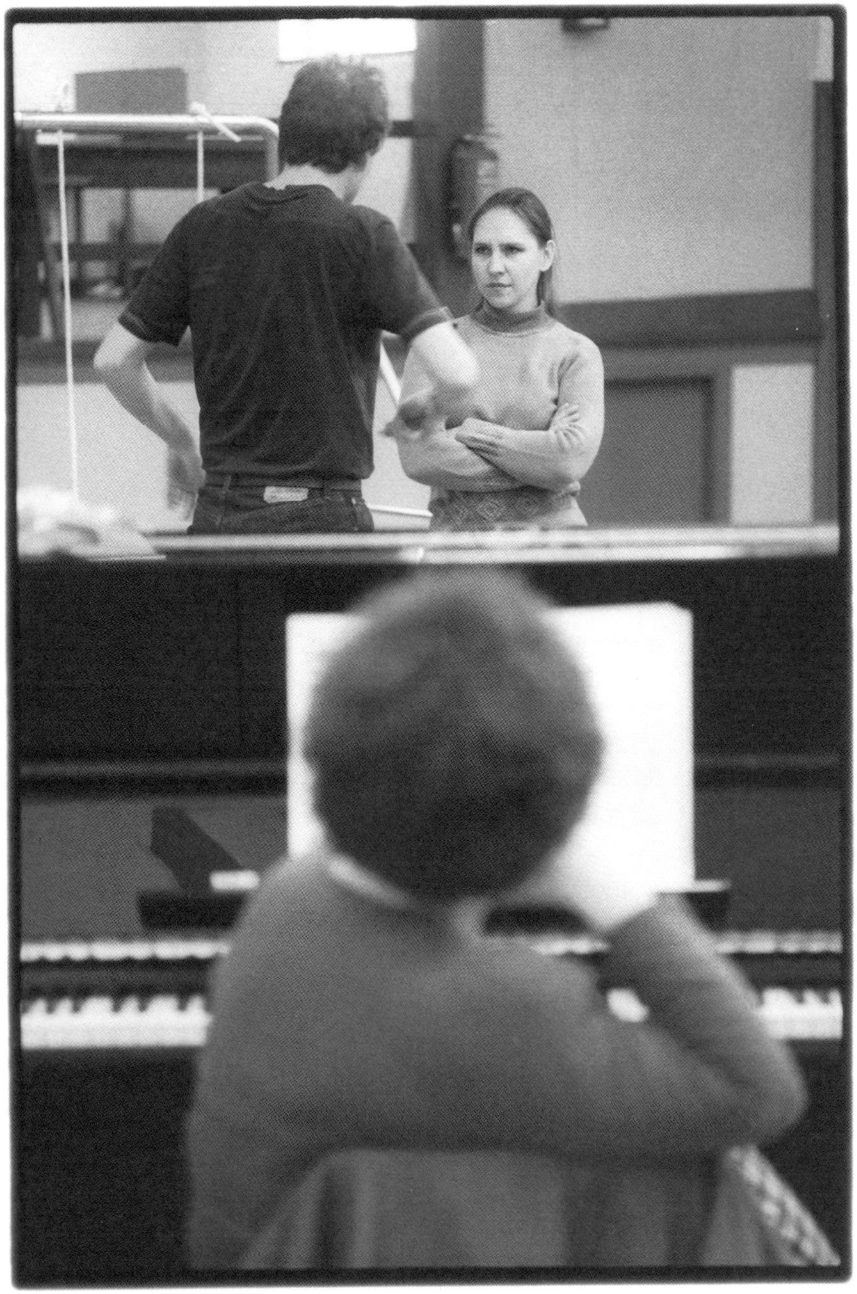

20

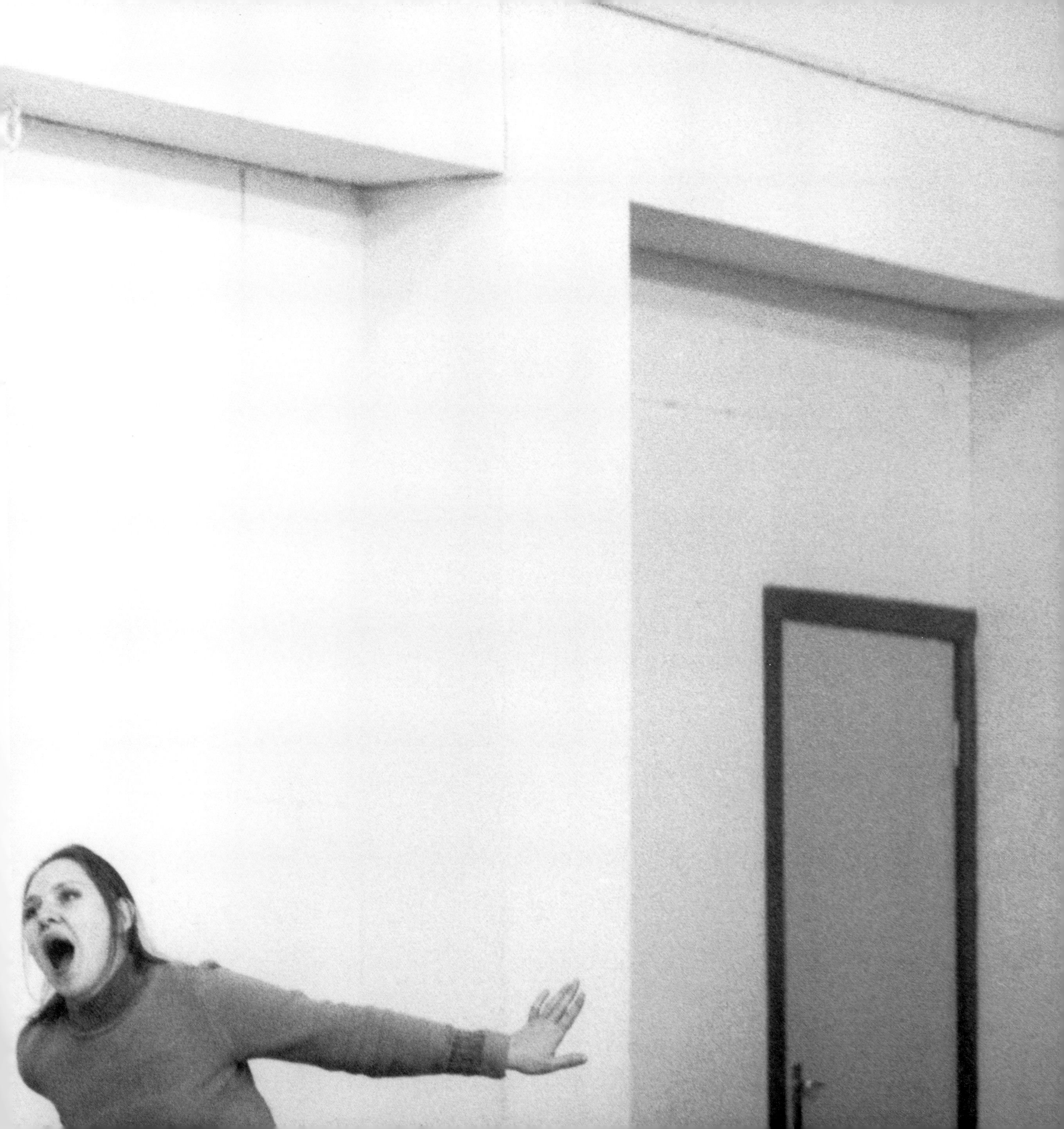

THE FRIARY Italian Bass Mirco Palazzi in rehearsal for *Jakobín* working with, from left to right, Director Michael McCaffrey, Stage Manager Ann Brodie and Conductor Alexandre Voloschulk. The addition to his girth formed an essential part of his costume!

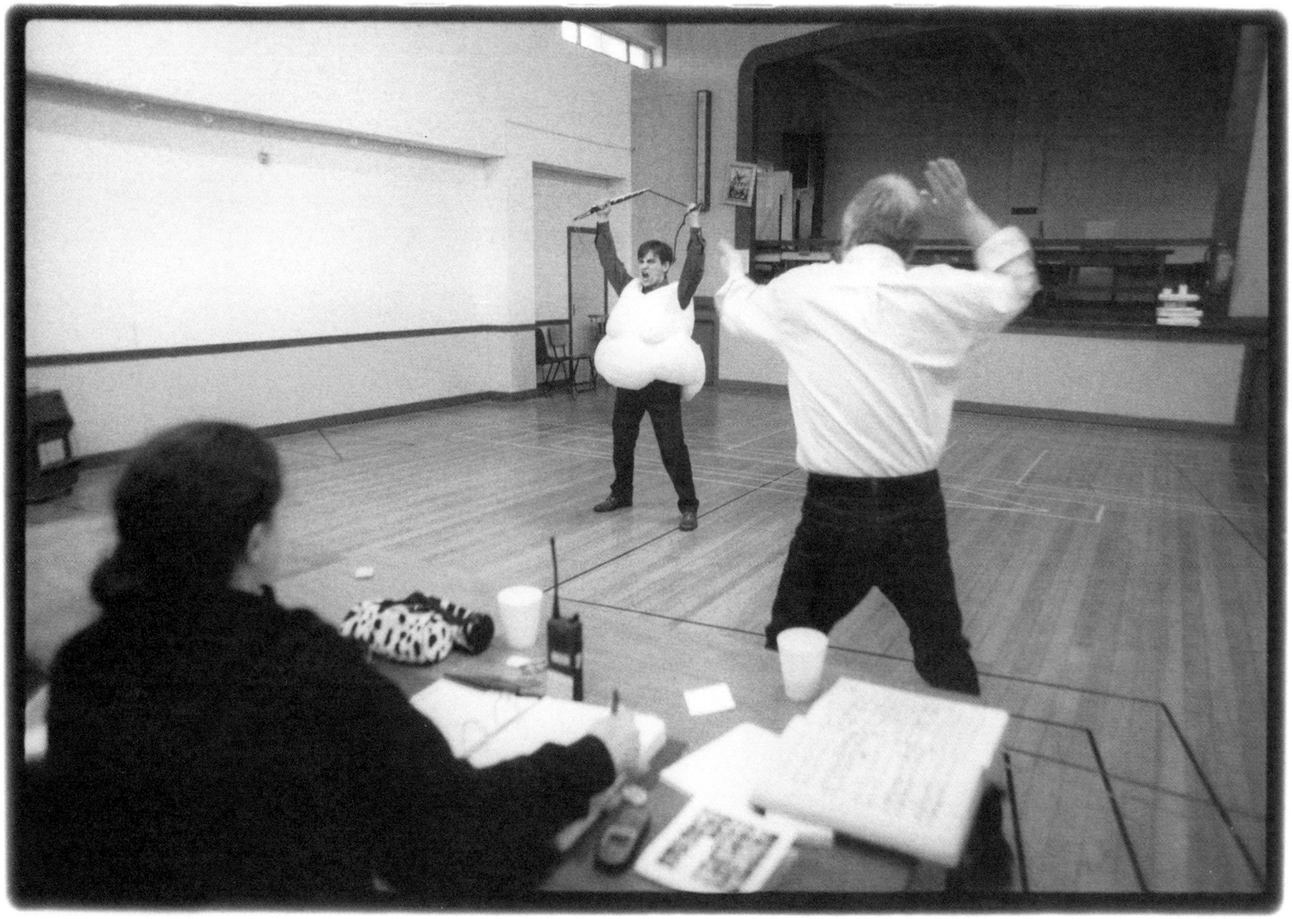

THEATRE ROYAL From the wings - a pause in rehearsals as the Stage Manager clarifies matters with the Director and the crew reset props for a repeat of the scene.

THEATRE ROYAL Supertitles were introduced at Wexford for the first time at the Fiftieth Festival and were warmly welcomed by audiences. Colin Cuthbert prepares to hang the secondary screen underneath the Circle during rehearsals.

Above, right & following page: **ON STAGE, THEATRE ROYAL** Giuseppina Piunti is directed by Fabio Sparvoli, Director of *Sapho* in rehearsals on stage at the Fiftieth Festival.

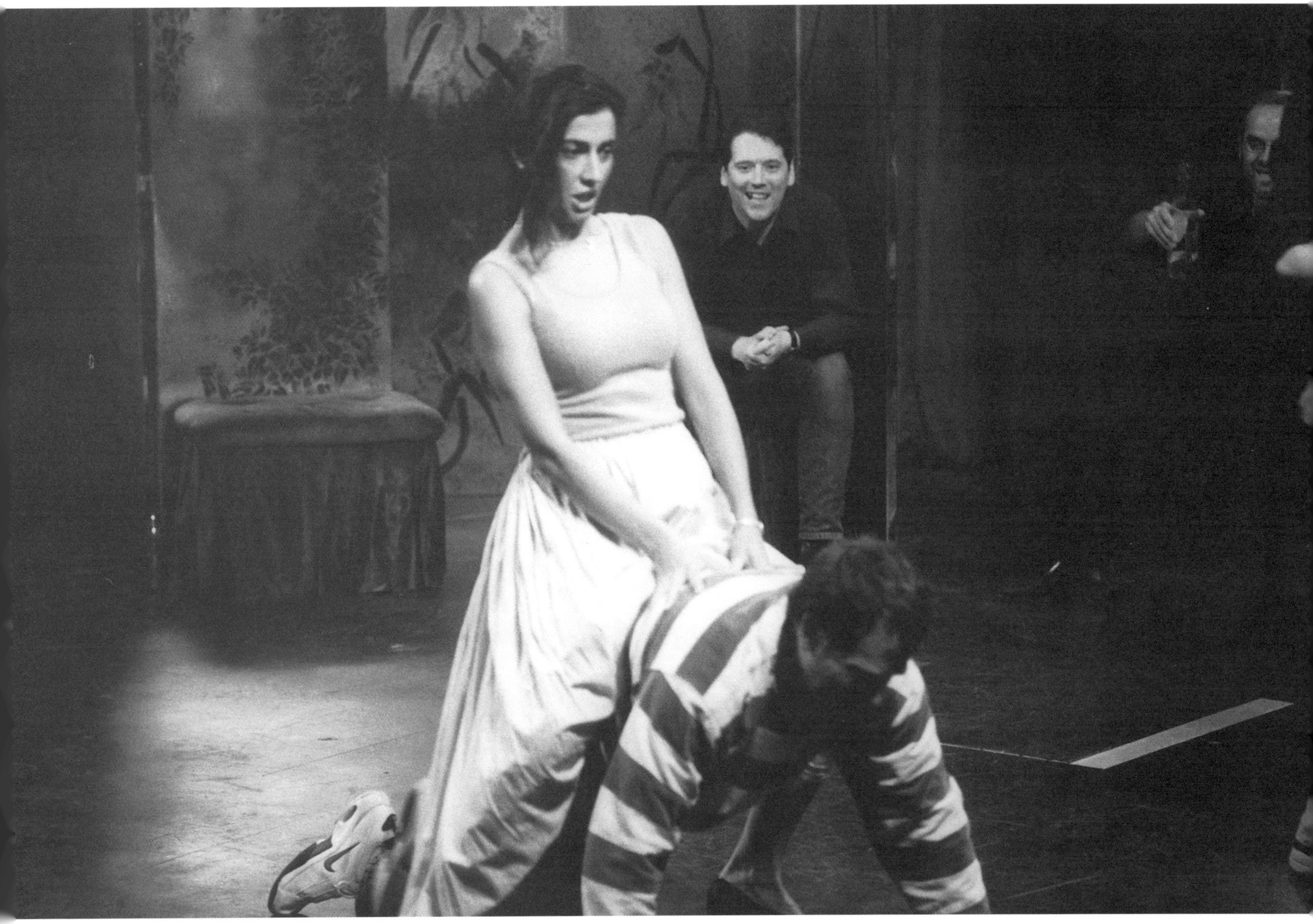

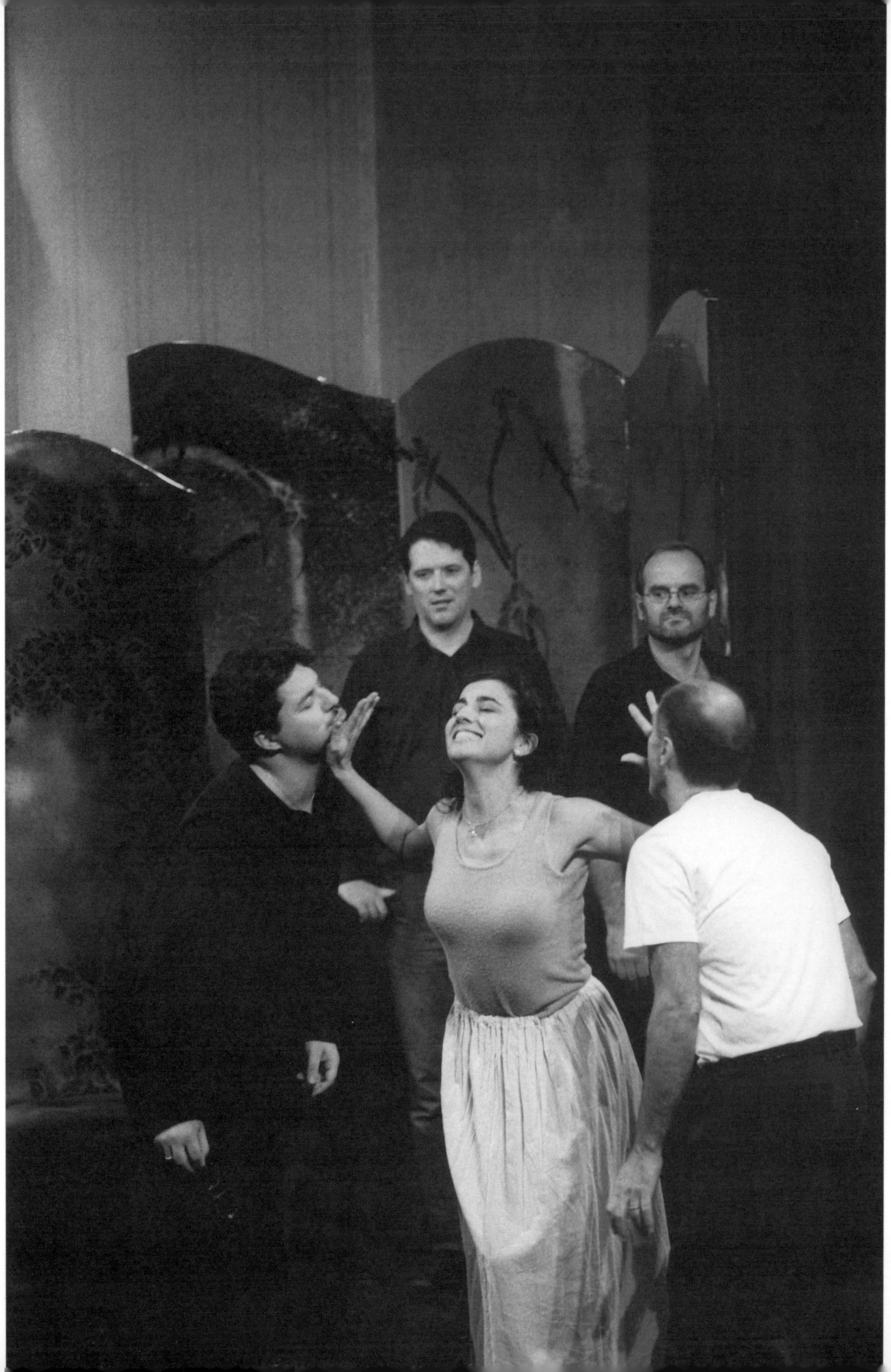

ST PETER'S COLLEGE Eithne Corrigan and Eanna McKenna both Wexfordians with Alexandre Voloschok the Russian Conductor, working on the production of *Jakobín* in rehearsal in St Peter's College Wexford.

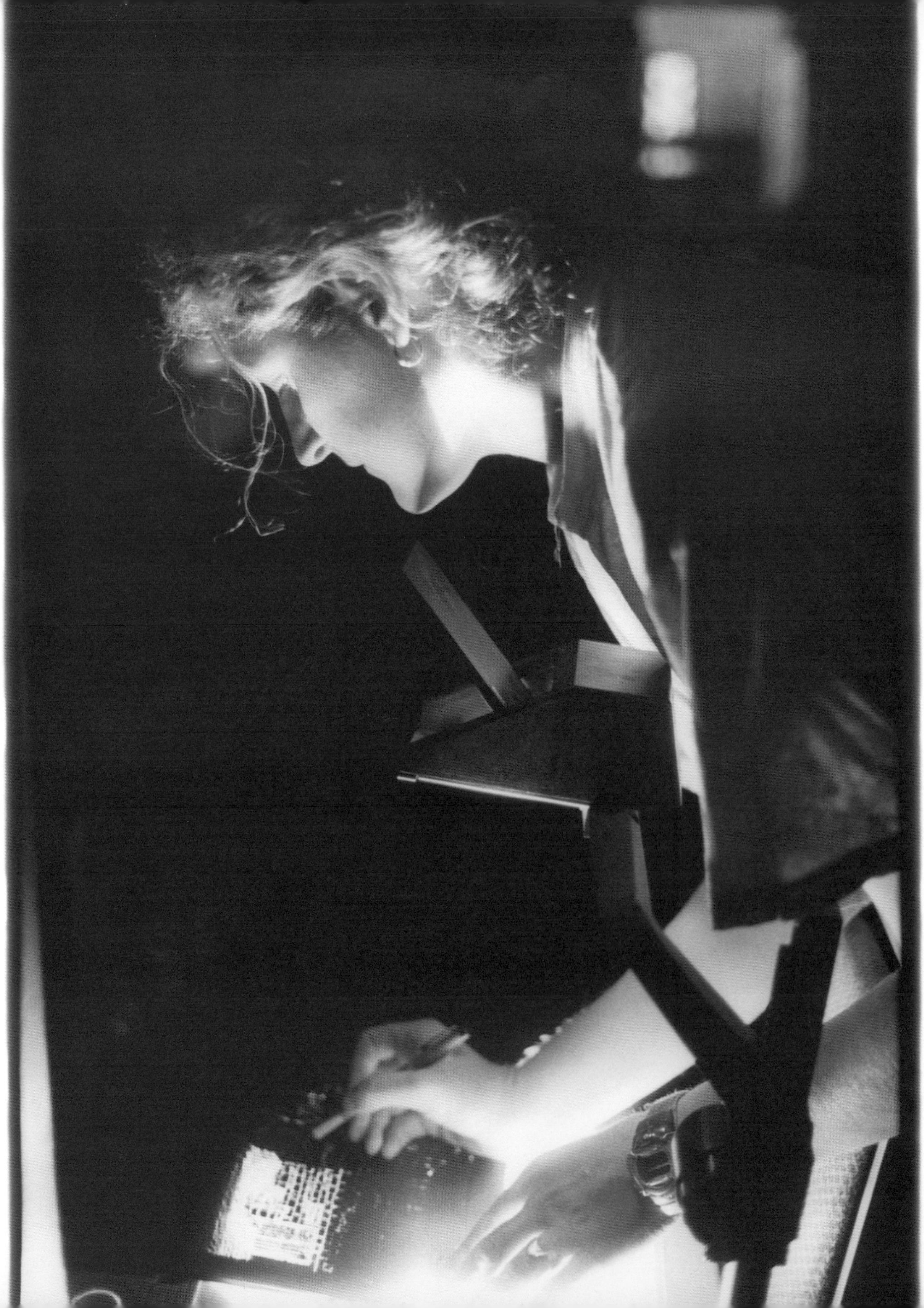

Left: **THE PEOPLE PROPERTY** Cristiana Aureggi, Props Supervisor, makes some final adjustments to pieces. Cristiana has been coming to Wexford to work at each Festival since 1996 and works from The Props House at No 23 High Street, a property purchased by the Festival in 1999.

Above: **THE BARRACKS** Mariana Panova rehearses the role of Terenkia in *Jakobín* in the Military Barracks in Wexford one of the rehearsal rooms used by the Festival.

GENERAL OFFICE 27 HIGH STREET The General Office of the Festival is a central part of the operation for the entire rehearsal and performance period assisting both members of the company and public. Pictured are Rebecca Keeling, General Office, Linda Molloy, PA and Phil Keeling, Festival Administrator.

FOYER, THEATRE ROYAL Festival Chief Executive Jerome Hynes and Chairman Ted Howlin have a word in the foyer. Ted has been Chairman since 1998. Prior to joining Wexford as its first Chief Executive Jerome was General Manager with Druid Theatre Company in Galway.

ON STAGE THEATRE ROYAL. Technical rehearsals continue after cast rehearsals sometimes well into the night, as efforts are made by all to adhere to the Wexford schedule of rehearsing and mounting three productions at the one time and opening them on consecutive nights. The photos in the foreground are of various scenes in production.

ON STAGE, THEATRE ROYAL A moment's pause for Stage Managers and crew during rehearsals.

OFFICES, 27 HIGH STREET Assistant Company Manager Oscar Cecchi discusses programme credits with Publications Editor Sue Hackett. The annual Festival programme has long been a souvenir publication with many people holding copies of all fifty programmes 1951 to 2001.

THE FESTIVAL LOUNGE, THEATRE ROYAL Artistic Director Luigi Ferrari in conversation with Mirco Palazzi the Italian Bass who played Fillip in *Jakobín* and went on to win a Bursary on the final night of the Festival. Luigi who is currently also General Director of the Teatro di Comunale di Bologna, has been working at Wexford since 1995. Also pictured is Volunteer and Local Music Supervisor Ger Lawlor.

ON STAGE, THEATRE ROYAL Wexford offers audiences the opportunity to see a different production each evening in The Theatre Royal over any three nights at the eighteen-day Festival. This involves crew working into the night striking one set and fitting up another for the following evening's production.

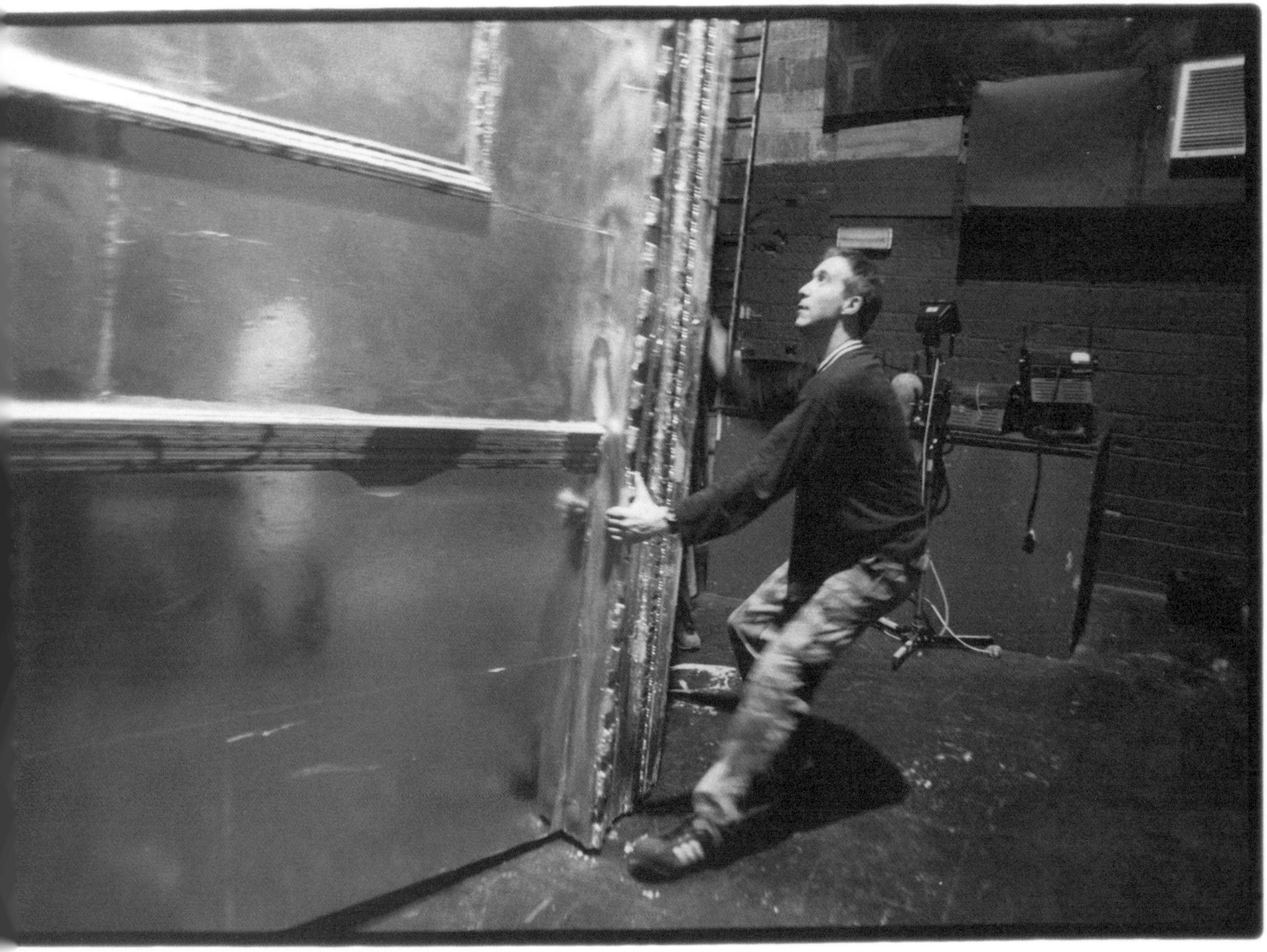

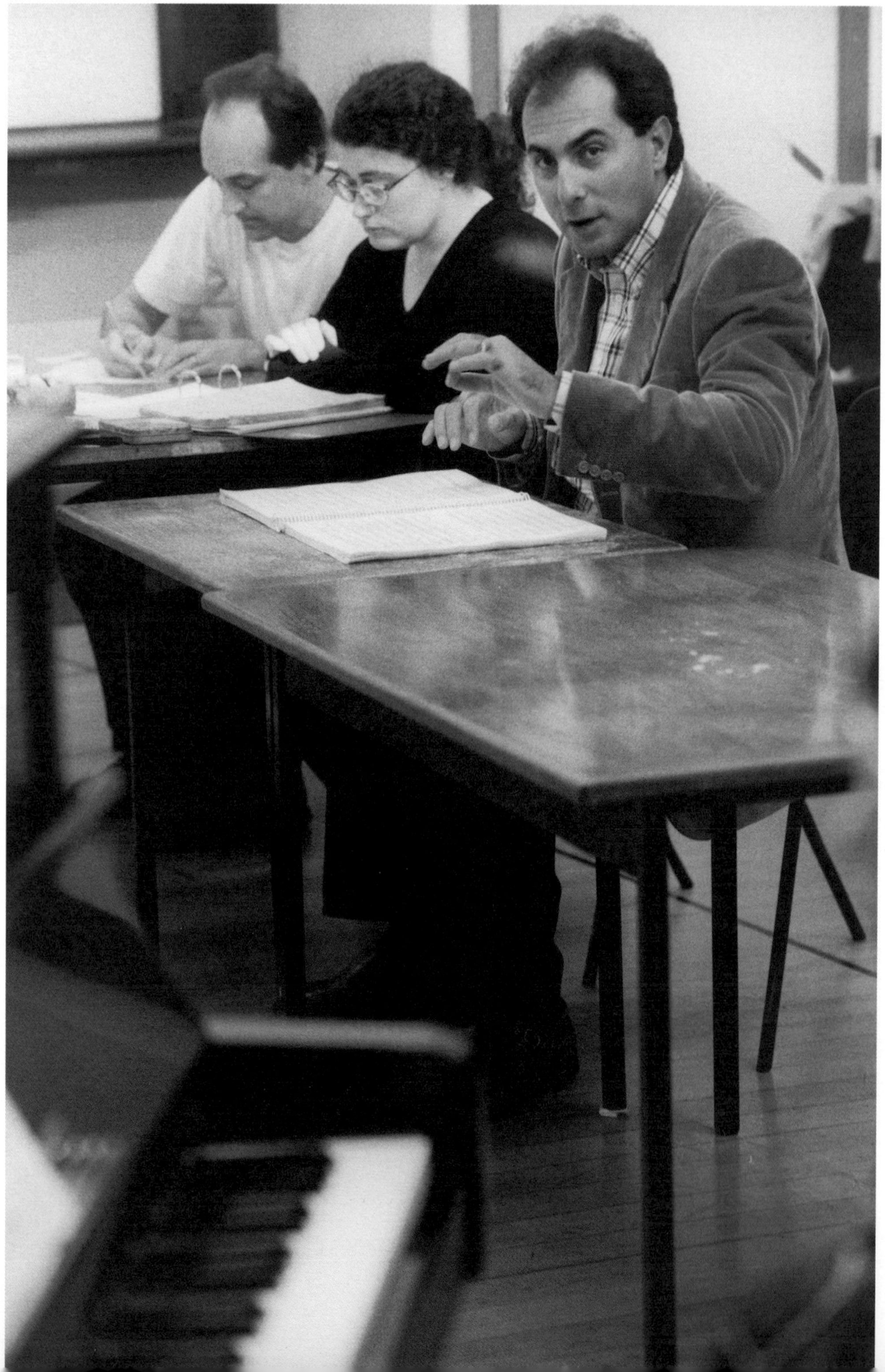

ST MICHAEL'S HALL *Left:* Conductor Daniele Callegari, with Stage Manager Vickki Madden and Director Thomas de Mallet Burgess, work in the rehearsal room on *Alessandro Stradella*. Daniele was Principal Guest Conductor from 1998 to 2001.

Above: Czech Bass Baritone František Zahradníček rehearses the role of Malvolio in *Alessandro Stradella*. This was his third appearance at the Festival having previously appeared in *Sarlatán* (1998) and in *Orleanskaya deva* (2000).

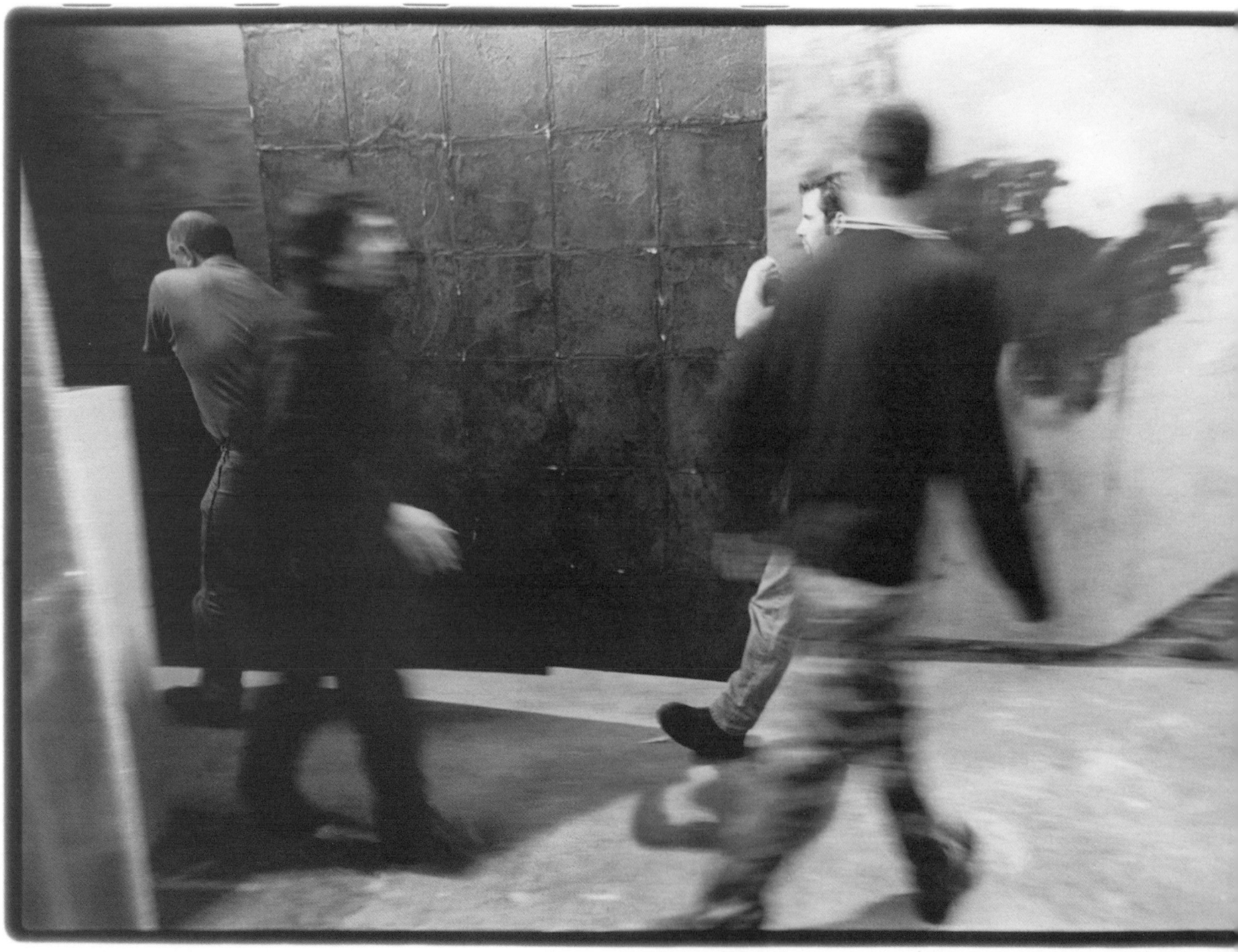

THE YARD, THEATRE ROYAL The arrival of the sets is an event eagerly awaited by members of the Wexford voluntary backstage crew. On left sets are moved into position. In the photograph on right with his hand on one of the gondolas from *Alessandro Stradella* is Nicky Cleary who leads the voluntary crew backstage and has worked on every Festival since 1953.

ON STAGE AND ON HIGH STREET With each production getting two days on stage followed by four days in a rehearsal room, the sets are struck during rehearsals every forty eight rather than every twenty four hours during performances. The gondolas for *Alessandro Stradella* arrive at the Theatre Royal from storage in The People Property.

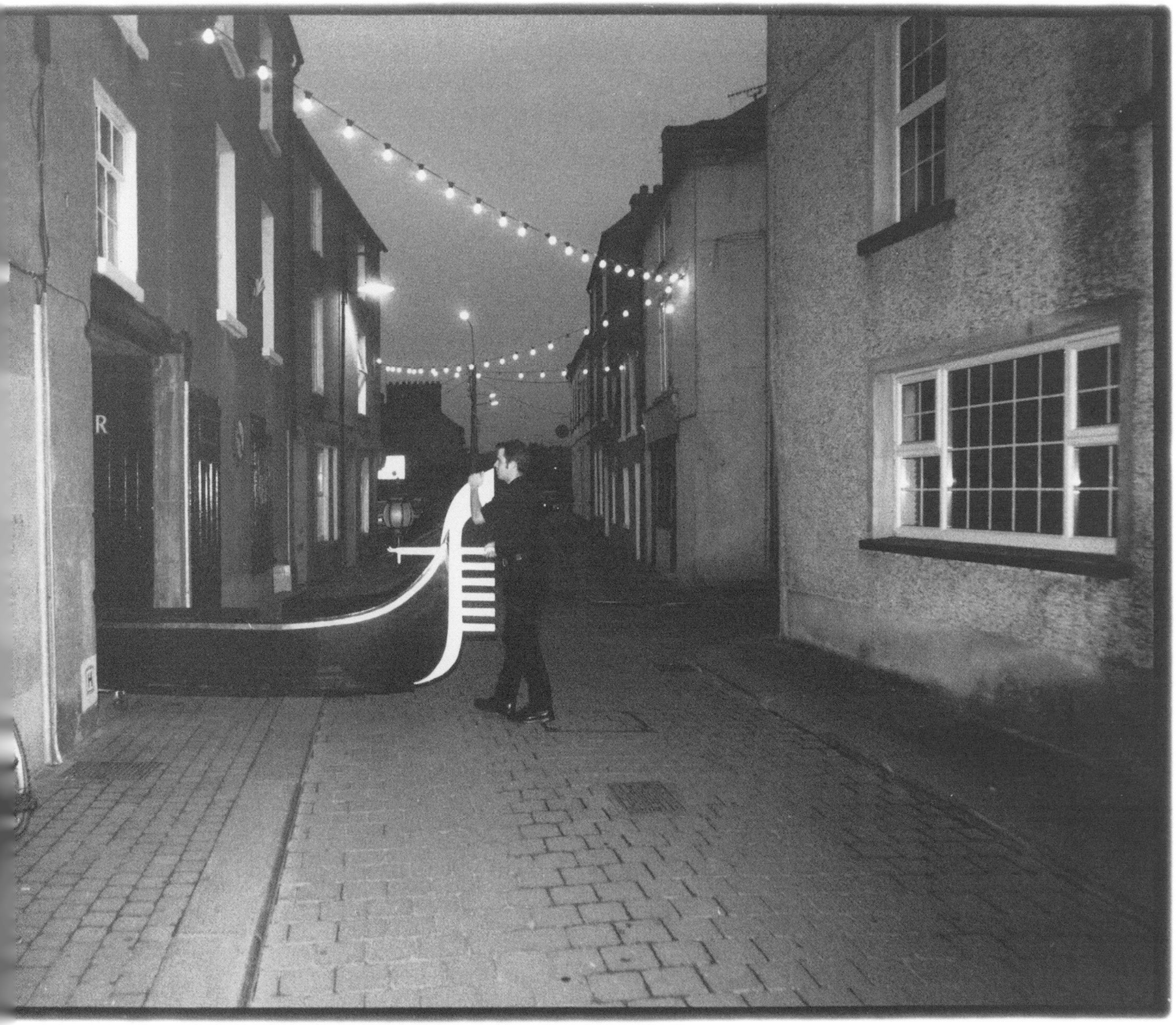
R

HIGH STREET Members of the orchestra gather at the Stage Door for the first rehearsal of the Fiftieth Festival. The orchestra, the National Philharmonic Orchestra of Belarus, were making their first appearance at Wexford at the Fiftieth Festival.

ROWE STREET CHURCH Members of The National Philharmonic Orchestra of Belarus shortly before performing Mozart's *Symphony No 41* and Prokofiev's *Classical Symphony* as part of their concert at Rowe Street Church.

Above: **THE DUN MHUIRE HALL** Daniele Callegari works in rehearsal with the National Philharmonic Orchestra of Belarus in The Dun Mhuire Hall shortly after their arrival in Wexford. Also pictured is Alena Kapustina, interpreter.

Right: **ROWE STREET CHURCH** Members of the National Philharmonic Orchestra of Belarus prepare for their appearance in concert at Rowe Street Church where they performed Mozart's *Symphony No 41* and Prokofiev's *Classical Symphony* as part of their contribution to the programme at the Fiftieth Festival.

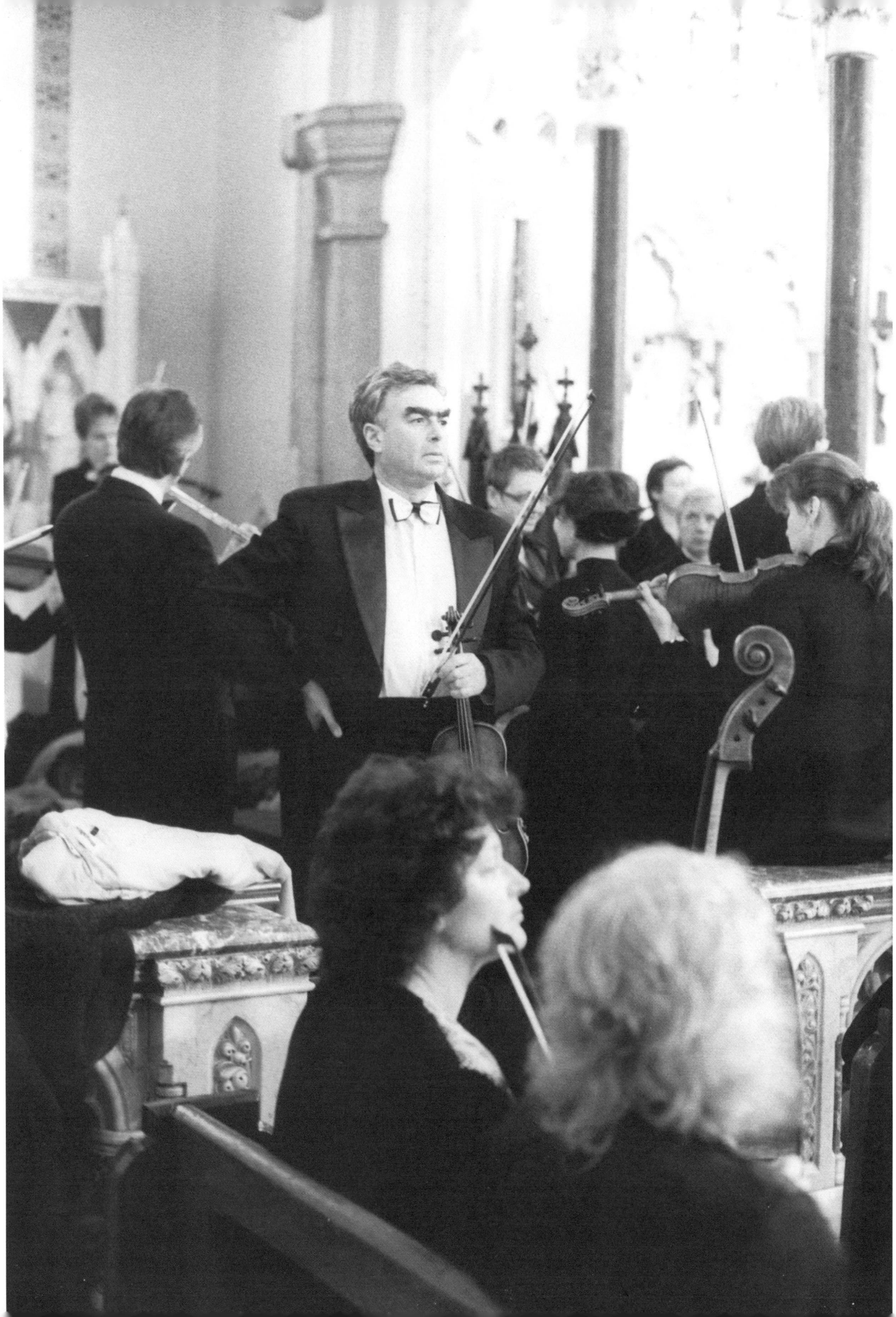

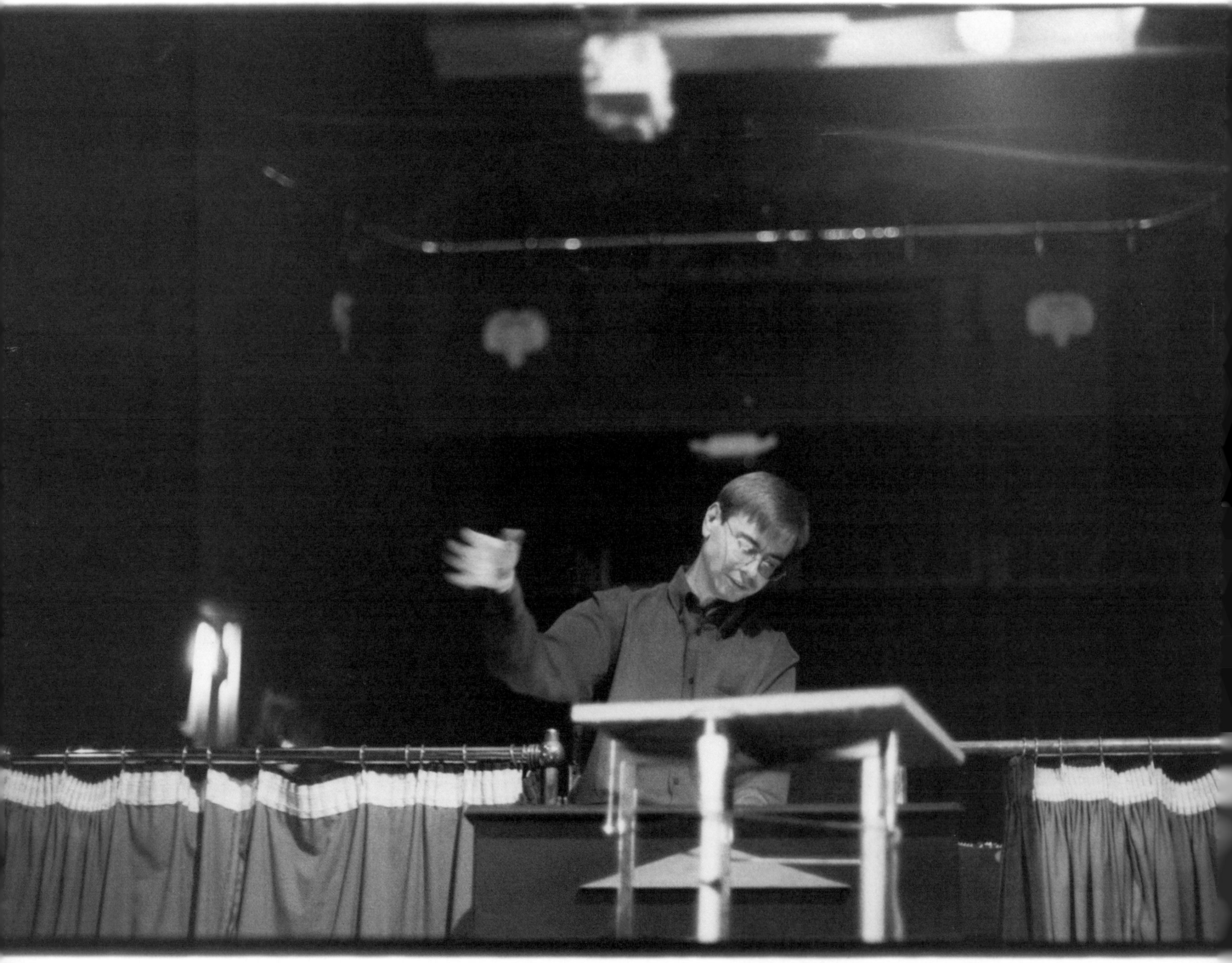

Above: **ST IBERIUS CHURCH** As part of the celebrations of the Fiftieth Festival BBC Radio Three broadcast their *In Tune* programme live from St Iberius Church before a live audience. Interviewees included Festival Artistic Director Luigi Ferrari (seen carrying a chair!) and Opera Director Rosetta Cucchi seen at the piano.

Left: **THE PIT, THEATRE ROYAL** Conductor Alexandre Voloschuk working with the cast in The Theatre Royal. The pit was extended in 1996 and can accommodate about fifty musicians.

ST PETER'S COLLEGE Stage Manager Anne Brodie in rehearsal with the principals and chorus of *Jakobín* in St Peter's College Wexford

OUTSIDE ROWE STREET CHURCH Members of the Wexford Festival Singers in final preparations for their appearance at the Choral and Orchestral Concert where they performed Bellini's *Mass in D major* and the Verdi *Quattro pezzi sacri*.

ON STAGE THEATRE ROYAL Director Michael McCaffrey working on stage with members of the cast and choreographer Lynne Hockney in rehearsals for the production of *Jakobín*.

QUAYSIDE Christoph Berthonneau, Founder and Artistic Director of the Fireworks specialists Groupe F, prepares his cues for the display which marked the opening of the Fiftieth Festival.

Above and right: **THE QUAYS** Technicians prepare the Quayside of Wexford for the Fireworks display which marked the Opening of the Fiftieth Festival. French company Groupe F, best known for their Millennium fireworks on the Eiffel Tower, worked with local company Nationwide Fireworks to provide a display which the press called *"a jaw-dropping spectacle that left a Wexford audience of 30,000 stunned"*.

Far right **THE CRESCENT, WEXFORD** The statue of John Barry, founder of the American Navy, towers above the crowds awaiting the Fireworks display on the quayside on the opening night.

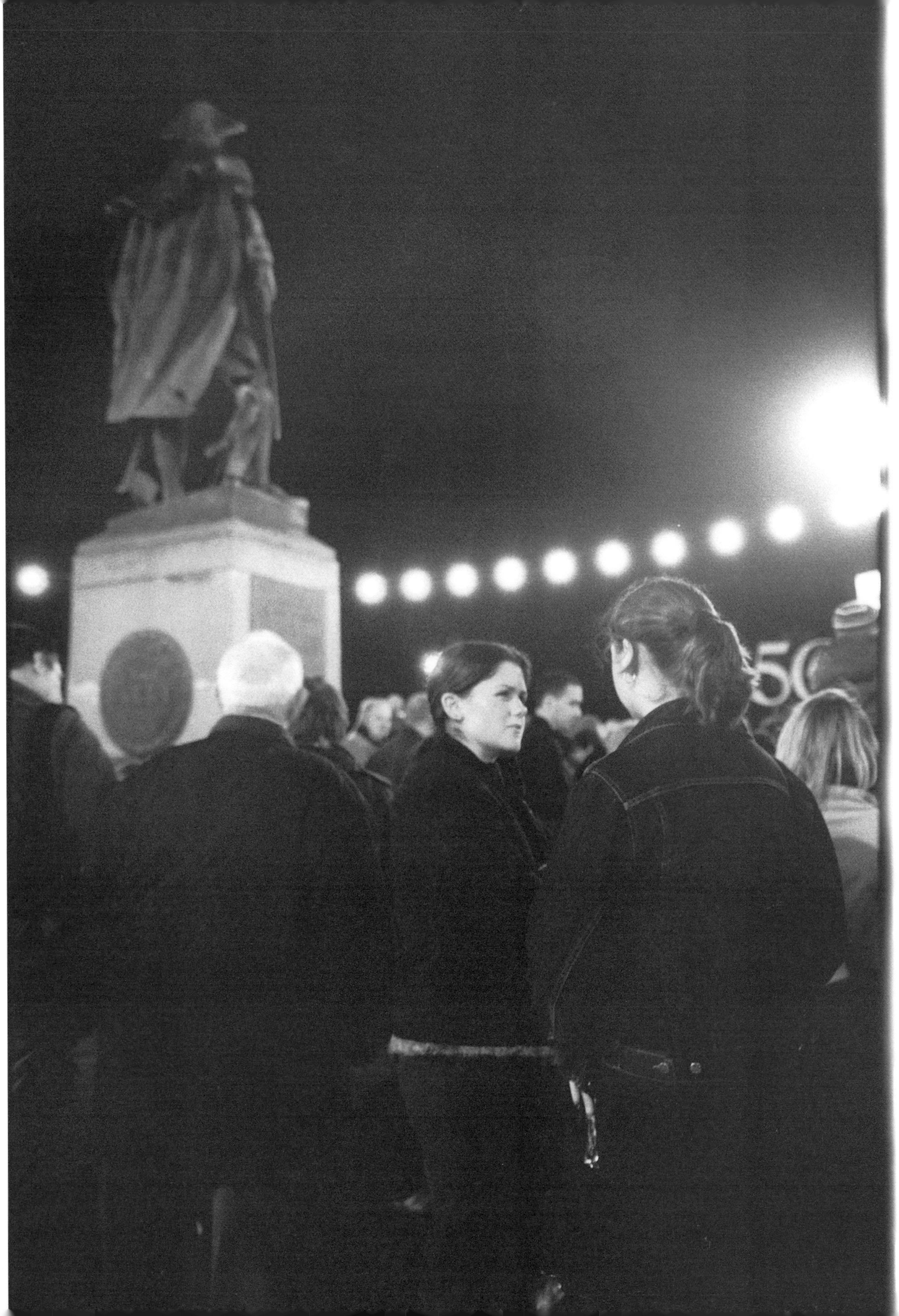
50

QUAYSIDE, WEXFORD Fireworks explode over the night sky above Wexford.

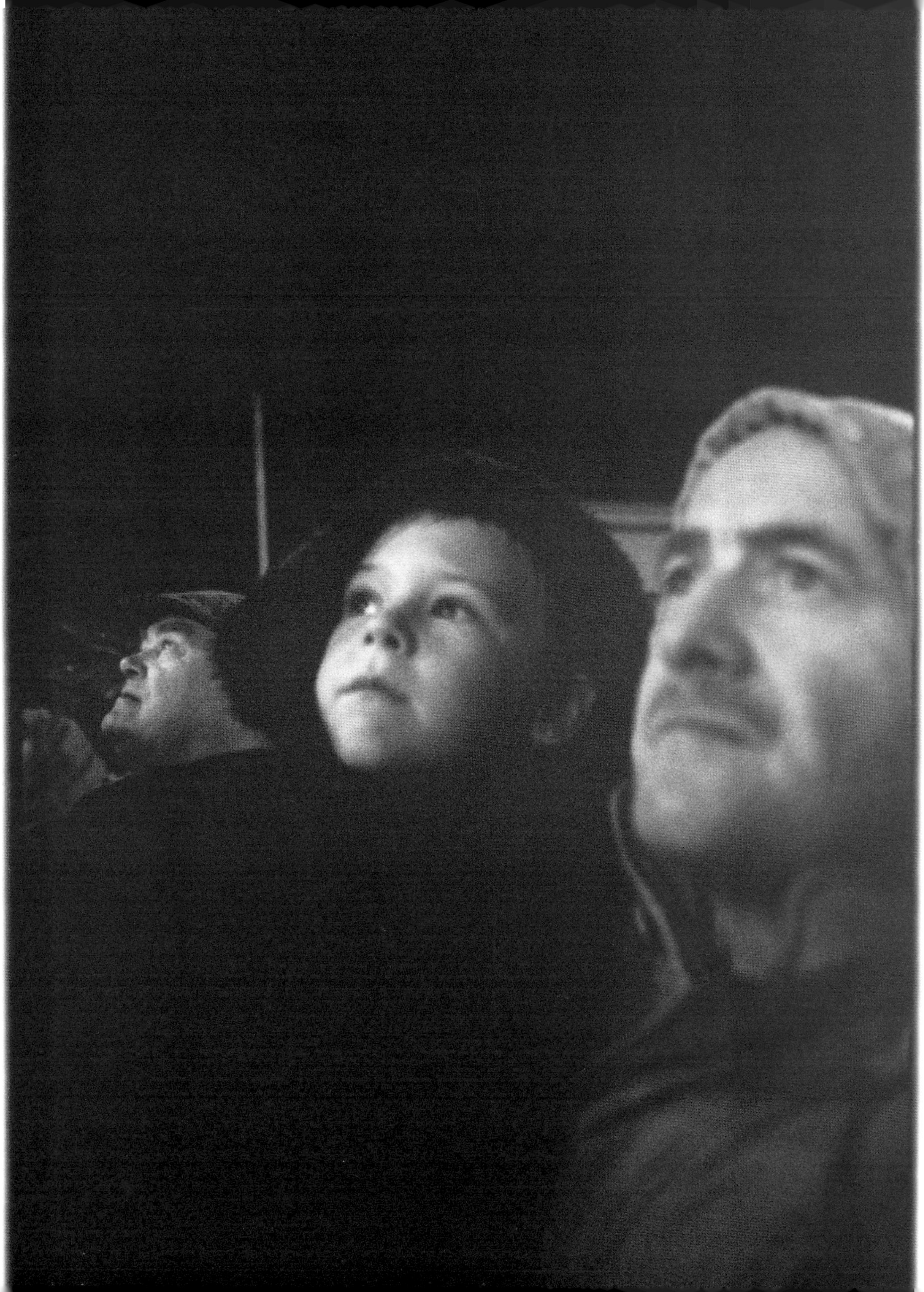

ON STAGE AND IN THE PIT, THEATRE ROYAL. Director Michael McCaffrey and Chorus Master Lubomir Mátl have a word during a break in rehearsals for *Jakobín*. Lubomir has been Chorus Master at Wexford since 1996. Meanwhile in the pit Repetiteur Robert Pechanec and Conductor Alexandre Voloschuk exchange notes.

ON STAGE Sara Palmer applies final details to the set of *Jakobín* prior to the first run-through in The Theatre Royal.

ST PETER'S COLLEGE Russian Conductor Alexandre Voloschuk working with cast members of *Jakobín* in St Peter's College Wexford, one of five rooms used for rehearsals by the Festival in the town.

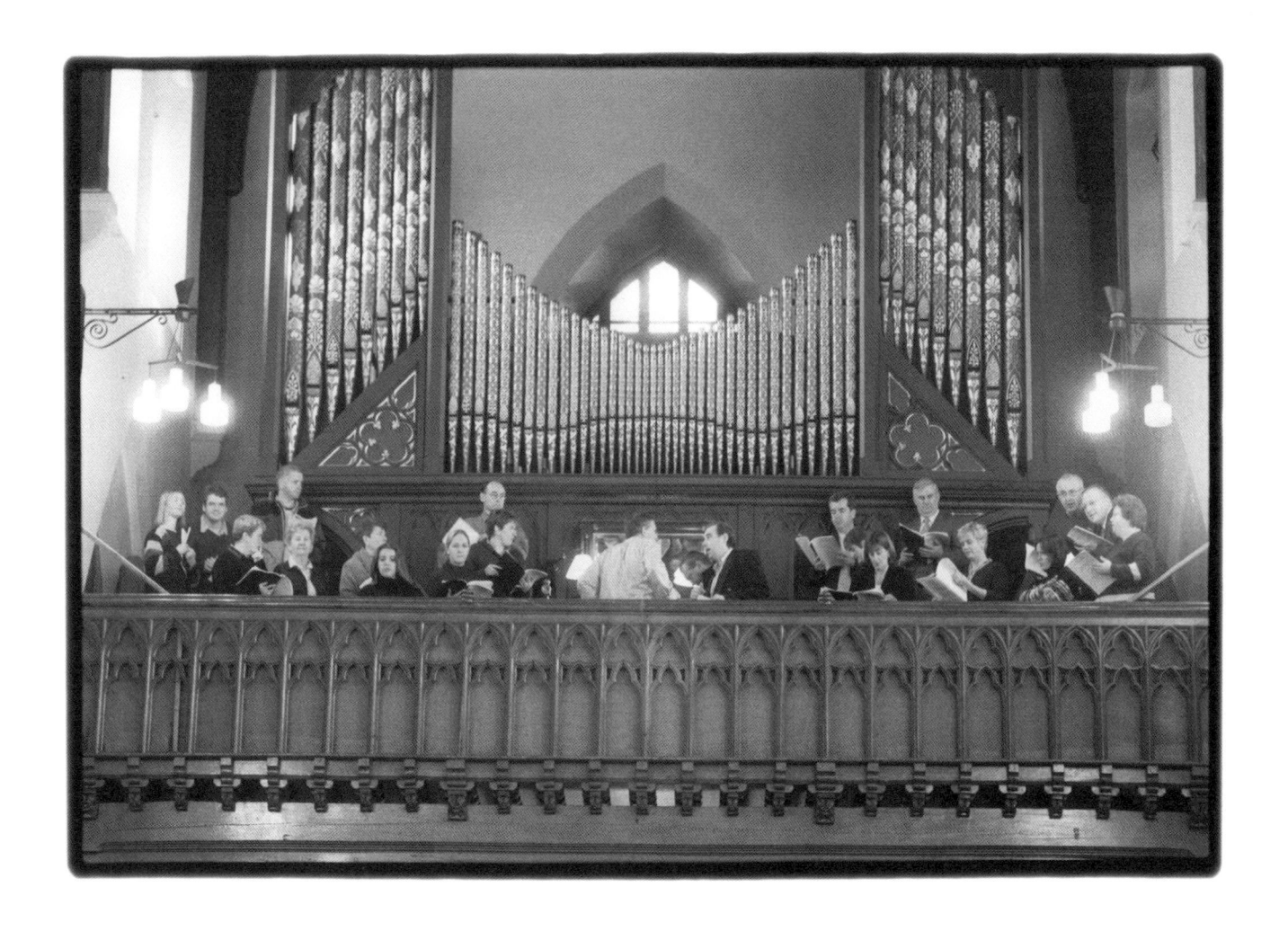

ROWE STREET CHURCH The Rowe Street Choir, conducted by Cyril Murphy, rehearse the Annual Festival Mass at Rowe Street Church. This has become an integral event for many people and involves soloists from the Festival participating in the service on the middle Sunday. There is a special Festival service in the Church of Ireland St Iberius Church on the first Sunday of each Festival.

THE FRIARY HALL Rosetta Cucchi directs her production of *Falstaff*, one of the Opera Scenes productions at the Fiftieth Festival. Rosetta who has worked at Wexford since 1995 also worked as Opera Manager at the Fiftieth Festival.

STALLS, THEATRE ROYAL Julia Frybert whose parents are both members of the Prague Chamber Choir has traveled to Wexford for five years now and attended school here while her parents worked on each Festival. At the Fiftieth Festival she joined the Young Wexford Singers to sing in the production of *Jakobín*.

FOYER THEATRE ROYAL Stella O Kennedy has a quiet word with Jerome Hynes. Stella has been a Volunteer in wardrobe since 1957 and has played a crucial role in that department at each Festival since then.

ST IBERIUS CHURCH Jermila Zilkova of The Prague Chamber Choir takes a final glance to ensure that all is in order before the concert by the Choir in St Iberius Church. The Choir has been a feature of the Festival since 1995. In the background is Rev Norman Ruddock, Rector of St Iberius Church.

THE FOYER THEATRE ROYAL The Dress Rehearsals at the Festival are sold strictly to Festival Volunteers and they queue, often for up to eight hours, to secure tickets. In the Box Office you can see Jim Golden former Chairman and longtime Festival Volunteer and Geraldine Dowler of the Box Office staff.

THE GREEN ROOM, THEATRE ROYAL Phyllis Foran and Collette Nolan, members of the Voluntary Canteen team take a rest during rehearsals for the productions in The Theatre Royal. The team provide essential sustenance for the almost one hundred and fifty artists performing at the Theatre Royal at each Festival.

DRESSING ROOMS, THEATRE ROYAL Anna Sollerman, Mezzo, during a costume fitting in the Dressing Rooms of The Theatre Royal.

THEATRE ROYAL FOYER Members of the voluntary Cloakroom team await the final curtain in The Theatre Royal. The entire Ground floor of Mrs. Breen's House (No. 21 High Street) doubles as a cloakroom pre and post performance and as a bar for the intervals, and was purchased by the Festival in 1992.

DRESSING ROOMS, THEATRE ROYAL Michaela Pertot, make-up artist, applies make-up in the Dressing Rooms prior to a performance during the Fiftieth Festival.

CLONARD COMMUNITY CENTRE The young performers prepare. To mark the Fiftieth Festival a special co-production of *The Raven King* – an opera for children and adults – was mounted by the Festival and Mary Immaculate College Limerick. It played to capacity audiences over three nights in Wexford and received three performances in Limerick.

SHOP WINDOW, CORNMARKET Wexford Chamber of Commerce organise a Festival Window Competition annually and invite a Designer from one of the Festival productions to judge. The competition helps to ensure that Wexford looks at its best for the tens of thousands of visitors to the area each year.

THE TALBOT HOTEL The Antique Dealers Fair has been running since 1975 and is held over the Bank Holiday weekend in The Talbot Hotel. One of the Friends parties coincides with the event and pictured is Nicky Furlong - who also conducts tours of Wexford during the Festival - at the Drinagh Antiques stand.

THE FERRYCARRIG HOTEL Opera Director Peter Ebert produced thirteen of the twenty six operas staged at Wexford between 1951 and 1965 and was invited to return to Wexford to give the Dr Tom Walsh Lecture in memory of the Festival founder. Since Dr Tom's death in 1988 this has become an annual tribute to him.

THE FERRYCARRIG HOTEL Gus Smith, critic and journalist with *The Sunday Independent* published a book to mark the Fiftieth Festival *Dr Tom's Legacy* and is pictured at the Ferrycarrig Hotel Wexford before attending the Dr Tom Walsh Lecture.

ST IBERIUS CHURCH The series of Lunchtime Concerts at the St Iberius Church attracted 100% occupancy in 2001 and featured key artists from the company. Lily Trappe a member of the Recitals Voluntary team awaits the arrival of the audience.

ROWE STREET CHURCH Tom Cirillo ready to call Daniele Callegari to the podium to conduct the National Philharmonic Orchestra of Belarus in concert at Rowe Street Church. Daniele was Principal Guest Conductor at Wexford from 1998 to 2001 and Tom Cirillo was Company Manager responsible for artistic scheduling for the 2001 Festival.

HIGH STREET WEXFORD Members of the audience walk along High Street on their way to the Theatre Royal for a performance. The street was cobbled by Wexford Corporation in 1999.

THEATRE ROYAL FOYER Three of the voluntary Front of House team take a breather during the first act of *Sapho* on the final night. Terry Ross, Joe Ryan and Paddy Foley are all living and working in Wexford.

FOYER, THEATRE ROYAL A newspaper photographer catches audience members in the foyer of the Theatre on the evening of a performance under the watchful eye of volunteer Tony Hynes.

Right: **HIGH STREET** The audience arrives at the Theatre for the opening night of *Sapho* on October 20th.

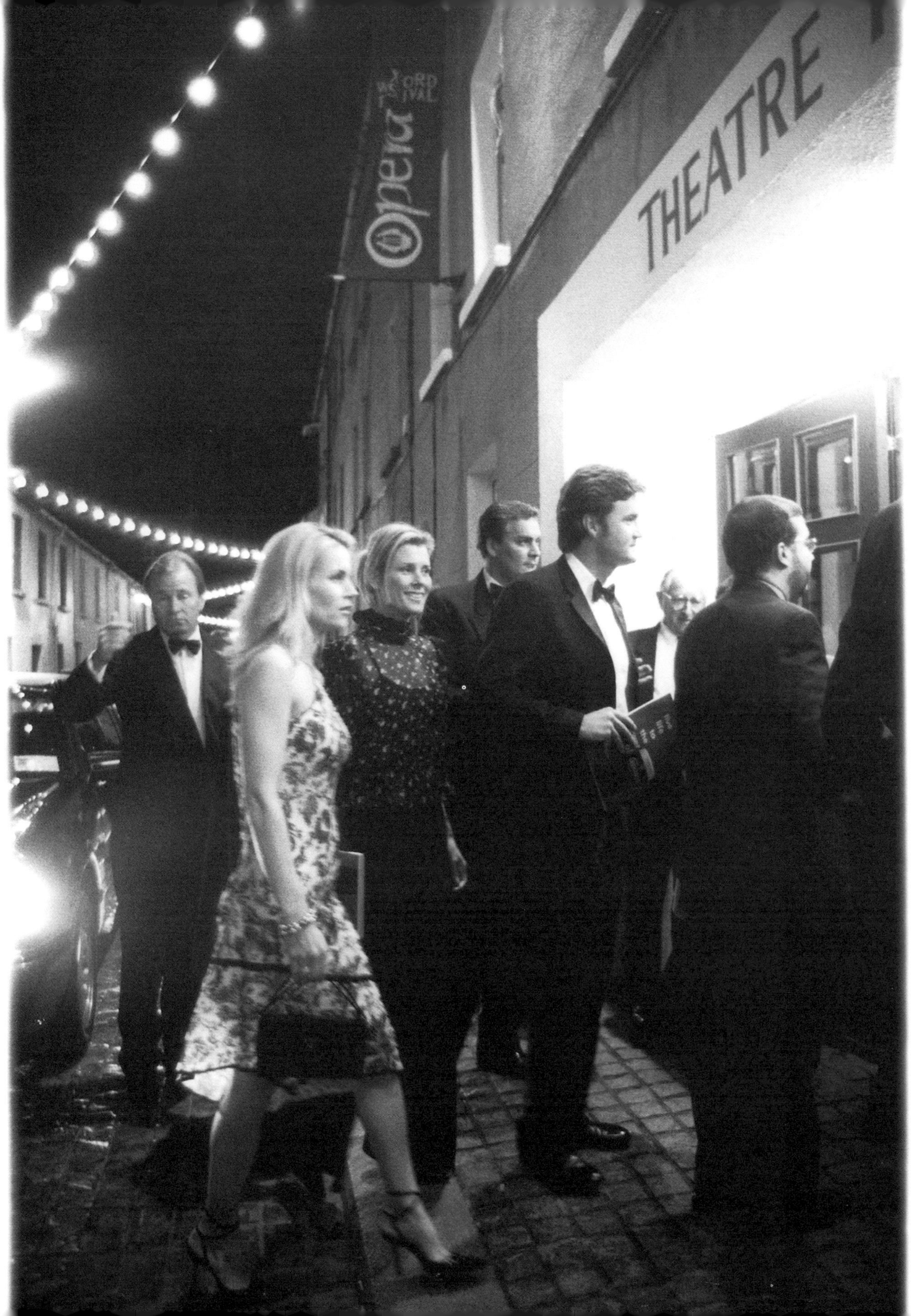
Opera
THEATRE

FOYER, THEATRE ROYAL *Above:* Audiences await a Dress Rehearsal in the foyer of the Theatre Royal. On left is Board member Mairead Furlong.

Right: A member of the audience prepares for the opera.

85

THE BOX, THEATRE ROYAL BBC broadcaster Sean Rafferty speaks to listeners worldwide in advance of the live broadcast of *Sapho* on November 1st. Sean has been a regular at Wexford for many years and presented his Radio Three programme In Tune from Wexford to mark the Fiftieth Festival.

HIGH STREET WEXFORD Members of the audience during an interval on High Street.

ON STAGE THEATRE ROYAL On the final night of each Festival the formalities include an address by the Festival Chairman, announcement of the Bursary Award Winners by the Chief Executive and the announcement of the following year's operas by the Artistic Director. This is followed by a rousing rendition by artists, staff, audiences, volunteers and crew of *Auld Lang Syne* bringing the curtain down on that year's Festival.

Photographer's note

I was delighted when Jerome Hynes asked me to photograph the Fiftieth Festival. I was born and live at 20 High Street opposite the Theatre Royal and so have been on familiar terms with it all my life. It was therefore a test to photograph the familiar and simultaneously exotic.

I wanted to reveal the essence of this remarkable event. And it really is a remarkable event to stage an opera, the talents of so many disciplines have to be combined, the set designers with the lighting designers, the conductors with the orchestra, the stage crew with the directors, the artists with the score, the administrative team with the entire operation - and everyone then has to function as a harmonious group! And Wexford produces three operas - or six if you include Operatic Scenes - at once!

My task then was to search through those elements to define in pictures that skill - whether it be through the camaraderie of the volunteers, the professionalism of the staff, the dedication of the singers or the patience of the orchestra. After many long hours attending rehearsals, watching people work and indeed getting to know the many people who go to make the event happen, I hope I have captured and can offer you a look at - in just over seventy images from the event - a stolen glimpse if you will.

The photographs were achieved with the help of Anna Papaconstantinou who stepped in and photographed some images when I was indisposed briefly. She is a New Zealander and studied photography at the Unitec School of Art and Design in Auckland.

Pádraig Grant 2002

Pádraig Grant is a photographer based in Wexford. He works with black and white materials and has exhibited widely throughout Ireland and abroad. He travels extensively most recently to Mexico, Iran, and throughout Africa and the Middle East and the resultant work has been the focus of many of his exhibitions.

Dr Tom Walsh
in the Theatre Royal

A Spirit of Confidence

Ian Fox considers 50 years of Wexford.

"For me it's a rather emotional evening really. Before I crossed last night I looked up to see when my grandfather had played and I find it was in 1835, a very long while back. He played in Waterford, Cork and Dublin and I'd like to think he'd played on the very boards on which I'm standing, but I don't think it's quite true and even under the romantic influence of Balfe I really don't think I can make that claim!".

Sir Compton Mackenzie was addressing the audience at the end of the first night of the Wexford Festival in 1951, having been introduced by the then Minister for Posts and Telegraphs, Erskine Childers, later to become President of Ireland. It had all started with a gramophone recital that Mackenzie, founder of the Gramophone magazine and a witty and erudite writer and speaker on music, had been persuaded to give to the Wexford Opera Study Circle in November 1950, during a visit to Ireland. The Chairman of the Circle, Dr. Tom Walsh, a medical practitioner and opera enthusiast, struck up an excellent relationship with him. Sir Compton suggested they should stage an opera in their little theatre instead of just listening to records. Not long afterwards, Dr Tom came across the programme for the 1949 Glyndebourne Festival during a visit to a London bookshop, and struck by the possibilities for Wexford, discussed the idea of a local version with his friends Dr. Des Ffrench, Eugene McCarthy, owner of White's Hotel, and Seamus O'Dwyer, a postal worker with an enormous operatic knowledge.

Mackenzie, described by Childers as "one of the last of the aristocratic rebels", was full of praise for Dr Tom's achievements: "Last year he talked to me, as we drove back to Dublin, and he told me about the future and his plans. He said: 'I suppose we'll have to do Balfe first'. But I know perfectly well he was thinking of the whole of *"The Ring"*, do you see! However, I'm giving him this – why don't you do *Sonnambula* next year?" The delighted Mackenzie became the Festival President, continuing up to his death in 1972.

Sir Compton Mackenzie speaking from the stage of the Theatre Royal after the first night of the first Wexford Festival, 4 November 1951. Behind him are James Cuthbert, Murray Dickie, Dermot O'Hara, Maureen Springer, Dr Tom Walsh, Angela O'Connor, James Browne, Statia Keyes, Nellie Walsh and the then Minister for Posts and Telegraphs, Erskine Childers, who was later President of Ireland.

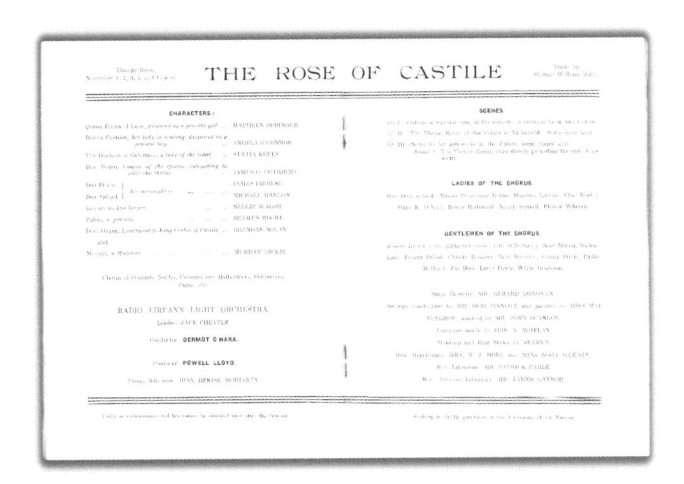

Centre spread of the programme book for the inaugural Wexford Festival Opera, 1951.

It took until 1954 for Bellini's opera to be staged, with Marilyn Cotlow as the sleep-walking Adina and Nicola Monti as her confused lover, Elvino. However Mackenzie had the right feel for the sort of opera suited to the modest scale of the Theatre Royal, particularly in those pre-rebuilding days. Despite falling short of their fund-raising, the group went ahead with a Festival of Music and the Arts from the 21st of October to the 4th of November, 1951, of which the highlight was a production of Balfe's *The Rose of Castile* on the first four nights of November. The opera was not in the repertory but had been a popular favourite in Victorian times. It had also been honoured by James Joyce, himself a tenor of some ability, in his great novel "Ulysses", with references to its music and a typically torturous Joycean pun. During the scene in the offices of the *Freeman's Journal*, in the "Aeolus" section, the journalist Lenehan poses a riddle: "What opera resembles a railway line?" and later provides the answer: "*The Rose of Castille* (sic). See the wheeze? Rows of cast steel.".

In the aftermath of the Second World War, the musical world was slowly pulling itself together again, particularly in Italy, and in those days it was possible to travel to Milan during one's Summer holidays and recruit a top-line team for that Autumn's Wexford season. Visitors like Nicola Monti, Afro Poli, Franco Calabrese and Paolo Pedani found themselves in the tiny Theatre, alongside such rising stars as Heather Harper, April Cantelo, Thomas Hemsley and Geraint Evans. The move away from well-known works to a menu of forgotten or neglected operas soon differentiated Wexford from other burgeoning festivals. Leading international critics, including the hugely influential Desmond Shawe Taylor, were quick to tell the world of the pickings, rich and rare, to be found on the banks of the River Slaney each Autumn. During its first decade Wexford offered an increasingly enthusiastic and knowledgeable audience such rarities as Lortzing's *Der Wildschütz*, with Heather Harper and Thomas Hemlsey, and Donizetti's *Anna Bolena*, with Fiorenza Cossotto and Plinio Clabassi, alongside such better-known, though at that time still obscure works, as *La Sonnambula*, as Mackenzie had

Paolo Pedani, Paolo Montarsolo, Dr Des Ffrench 1957.

La Sonnambula artists in the Bullring 1954. (L-R) Gwyn Griffiths, Halinka de Tarczynska, Franco Calabrese, Marilyn Cotlow, Nicola Monti, Thetis Blacker, Daniel McCoshan, John Clifford.

(L-R) Peter Ebert, Dr. Tom Walsh, Dr. Des Ffrench and Elvina Ramella.

Sir Alfred Beit

suggested, and *Rossini's L'Italiana in Algeri,* with April Cantelo and Paolo Montasarlo. Bryan Balkwill, Charles Mackerras and John Pritchard were among the young conductors, working with such subsequently famous producers as Peter Ebert and Anthony Besch, and designers like Osbert Lancaster and Michael MacLiammoir. The results for their day were electrifying and the Festival was soon attracting leading operatic talent, both new and established, managers in search of new voices and audiences of opera fanatics from around the World.

For its first season in the Theatre, the Festival Committee had thousands of paper chrysanthemums made to cover the worst of the many cracks in the building. Having acquired the Theatre in the 1950s, the Council, with its limited resources, could only work slowly on cleaning and restoration. As the success of this madcap venture gathered momentum, plans were drawn up to build a new opera house; one scheme would have moved it to the north side of the river at Ferrybank, beside the main bridge, but building costs at around £50,000 were too high. Instead, a reconstruction appeal was launched with help from the Irish Tourist Board. Toward the end of the decade, Sir Alfred Beit, who had settled in Russborough House in County Wicklow, became involved in the Festival. He persuaded the Gulbenkian Foundation to provide £15,000, a considerable sum in those days, as the main source of funding. The scale of the work prevented a 1960 season taking place, so the Festival is always one year younger than its calendar date suggests. The year 1961 also saw the establishment of the Friends of the Wexford Festival under the guidance of the redoubtable Lt. Col. David Price.

The re-opening was marked by a production of Verdi's *Ernani* in September 1961, produced by Peter Ebert with designs by Reginald Woolley. Problems in obtaining the Radio Éireann Light Orchestra (now the RTÉ Concert Orchestra) led to the involvement of the Liverpool Philharmonic under Bryan Balkwill for this one season. The next year the Radio Éireann Symphony Orchestra (now the National Symphony Orchestra of Ireland) moved into the pit, a role it filled up to 2000. The 1962 *L'Amico Fritz* (Mascagni) brought the talented young Irish

Nicola Monti, Bernadette Greevy, Paolo Pedani and Veronica Dunne in *L'Amico Fritz* 1962.

Teas and coffees backstage at the interval 1959

Fra Diavolo 1966 Nigel Douglas, Anna Reynolds, Renato
Ercolani, Ugo Benelli, Alberta Valentini

singers Veronica Dunne and Bernadette Greevy to international notice, in a cast including Nicolai Monti and Palo Pedani. Other distinguished names from the 1960s included Mirella Freni (Bellini's *I Puritani* 1962), Margarita Rinaldi (Donizetti's *Don Pasquale* 1963) and a subsequent Wexford favourite, Ugo Benelli (Auber's *Fra Diavolo* 1966). A youthful Philip Langridge appeared in a small role in *La Traviata* in 1965; when he returned in 1975 for Cavalli's *Eritrea*, an emerging Dublin mezzo-soprano was in the cast, Ann Murray, and the encounter led to their marriage.

A sample of the kind of fare being offered in the Sixties can be seen in the 1964 programme, when, as well as the three operas (Donizetti's *Lucia di Lammermoor*, Rossini's *Il Conte Ory* and Stanford's *Much Ado About Nothing*), there was the Festival Forum, then a popular annual event, with Huw Weldon featuring on that year's panel, plus Handel's *Acis and Galatea*, performed by the Guinness Choir. The remarkable Dublin University Players staged one of their famous late-night revues and there was just one chamber music recital. It was a small calendar compared to today's busy programme. For social activities there was a Festival Ball, while an advertisement for a leading hotel provided a salutary headline, bidding us all to "*Wine... dine... and be gay (All are welcome!)*".

The 1965 production of Massenet's *Don Quichotte* brought veteran bass Mirsolav Cangalovic for a famous appearance as Cervantes's batty Knight. It also saw the arrival of a young conductor from Prague, Albert Rosen. This started a long relationship with Wexford and then the Symphony Orchestra. Following that auspicious debut, a production still much talked about among the older Wexford cognoscenti, he went on to conduct more Wexford productions than anyone else, eighteen all told. Rosen was later appointed Principal Conductor of the RTÉ Symphony Orchestra and was Conductor Laureate at the time of his death in 1997.

Dr Tom continued to exercise his skills into the 1960s but made the unexpected decision to step down after the 1966 season. The post was advertised and Walter Legge, the famous EMI record producer, was a surprise candidate. However, Legge had a heart attack (though he recovered and lived on until 1979) and withdrew. Instead a young, 26-year-old former Trinity College student, Brian Dickie was appointed; he had been with the Glyndebourne Touring company and brought a fresh approach to programme planning. A new era of outstanding

Miroslav Cangalovic in the title role of *Don Quichotte* 1965

singing emerged, together with an exploration of fresh repertory, providing Wexford's first operas in Russian *(Glinka's Ivan Susanin)* and Czech *(Janáček's Katá Kabanová)*, plus a new emphasis on French compositions. Christine Eda-Pierre arrived from the Paris Opera for Delibes's *Lakmé* in 1970, returning the next year for Bizet's *Les Pêcheurs de Perles* It is hard to realise today that both these operas were considerable rarities thirty years ago. Among the new names to be spotted in the smaller roles was that of tenor Dennis O'Neill, who made his Wexford debut in 1973 as a messenger in *Ivan Susanin*.

A feature of these years was the film season, a valuable asset in those pre-videotape days, held in the local cinemas. In 1968 there was a Marilyn Monroe season, while other years were devoted to screenings of films by Passolini, Bergman and Milos Forman. Operatic movies and arts documentaries were also featured in these cinematic ventures. In 1969 the Festival experienced its first contemporary opera when Irish National Opera brought its production of James Wilson's *Twelfth Night* to the Festival. A second Wilson creation, *The Pied Piper of Hamelin*, was seen in a puppet opera version the same year. The Northern Sinfonia paid a visit to the Festival in 1970 under the baton of Rudolf Schwarz and the 1973 programme added a list of sporting events, ranging from a Beagle Meeting to Crab Fishing. The extensive supporting actives now feature in a busy Fringe Festival which runs alongside the main event and for which a separate programme is published each year.

• • •

With his remarkable success, particularly in one so young, Dickie was soon being head-hunted and was persuaded to return to Glyndebourne. His successor in 1974, Thomson Smillie, had been Publicity Officer at Scottish Opera and his Celtic charm provided a notable contrast to the often abrasive Dickie. He maintained the three-opera format, for the first time defining them as comprising a singers' opera, a comedy and a thinking piece. Massenet was much neglected at the time and he staged *Thaïs* in his first season, starting a remarkable series of his operas over the years since; *Saffo*, the Festival's seventh Massenet opera, was staged in 2002. One of the most memorable productions took place in 1976: Britten's *The Turn of the Screw*, directed by Adrian Slack, designed by David Fielding and conducted by Albert Rosen, giving a young Wexford boy soprano, James Maguire, the opportunity to shine in the key role of Miles. Smillie also brought the great buffo, Sesto Bruscantini, to Wexford for a memorable triple bill in 1977.

Sergei Leiferkus in Massenet's *Grisélidis* 1982

He gave an hilarious performance in Cimarosa's one-man piece *Il Maestro di Capella*, and was equally delightful in Ricci's *La Serva e l'Ussero* and Pergolesi's *La Serva Padrona*. Bruscantini returned in 1979 for the Ricci brothers' comedy *Crispino e la Comare*. In 1979 Smillie accepted a post in Boston and left the Festival, he later ran Kentucky Opera for many years. He was succeeded by producer Adrian Slack who remained for three years.

The old Assembly Rooms in the Cornmarket were extensively restored and re-opened as an arts centre in 1974. The Festival subsequently passed over many of its non-musical activities to this new facility and, under its own full-time management, the Wexford Arts Centre has become the home of a wide range of art exhibitions, concerts, drama and late night events in the years since, as well as providing a vibrant year-round service for the arts locally. Celebrity recitals in the Theatre Royal in these years included concerts by Sena Jurinac (1975), Frederica von Stade (1976) Kerstin Meyer (1977), Benjamin Luxon (1978), who performed both of Schubert's great song-cycles, *Die Schöne Müllerin* and *Die Winterreise* on the one afternoon, and Bernadette Greevy and Ugo Benelli in the same year (1981). Other Festival visitors from the seventies and early eighties included the RTE Academica Quartet with the young Mariana Sirbu as leader; now a distinguished international soloist, she was appointed principal Guest Director of the Irish Chamber Orchestra early in 2002 and returns to Ireland after many years. The first of the Young Irish Artists concerts took place in 1980 and pianist John O'Conor started his long association with the Festival, presenting a recital and playing with the Academica Quartet. He was to become a frequent soloist and accompanist at the Festival, appearing with such artists as Günter von Kannen, Sergei Leiferkus, Ugo Benelli and Yan Pascal Tortelier.

In 1981 the Festival received a remarkable accolade from a regular visitor and fan, Bernard Levin. He had been commissioned by the BBC to present a series of radio talks on his favourite music festivals. This was followed by a book *Conducted Tour* (Jonathan Cape) featuring his choice of the twelve best music (not just opera) festivals in the world. Wexford suddenly found itself rubbing shoulders with Salzburg, Glyndebourne and Bayreuth. While poking some wry fun at the Festival, as he did with the other eleven, Levin was unreserved in praise. Quoting a friend's comment (that it is the world's best children's party for adults), he adds: "she has seen into the heart of Wexford's mystery, for we are all children at Wexford, innocent and delighted, accepting joy as the natural order of the universe", and he concludes "Tom Walsh, thirty years ago, little knew what he was starting. Or perhaps he did…here in Wexford his monument stands, a festival of music and joy to refresh the spirits, brighten the sky and flavour the year". Levin also contributed a moving obituary in the London Times in November 1988 on *Doctor Tom's final curtain*: "Doubt not that he feasts in heaven this night, with Mozart on one side of him and Hippocrates on the other, and a glass of good red wine in his good right hand".

Adrian Slack's successor in 1982 was Elaine Padmore. She had been a BBC radio opera producer and had supervised a number of broadcast transmissions of the productions for BBC Radio Three. Her thirteen-year reign, only two shorter than Dr. Tom, brought a wide spectrum of music and singers with many remarkable productions. Marschner's *Hans Heiling* caused quite a stir in 1983 in Stephen Pimlott's production, designed again by David Fielding, and introduced Sergei Leiferkus to audiences outside Russia. Raul Gimenez, Cynthia Clarey, Bruce Ford, Curtis Rayam, Kristine Ciesinski, Karen Notare, Alison Browner and Bernadette Greevy are just some of the singers who thrilled audiences during her era. Other outstanding productions included new-comer Francesco Zambello's two stagings: *L'assedio di Calais* (Donizetti) in 1991 with Alison Browner and *Cherevichki* (Tchaikovsky) in 1993. In the latter Alexander Anissimov made his Irish debut, going to become Chief Conductor of the National Symphony Orchestra of Ireland and now the Orchestra's Conductor Emeritus. There were Patrick Mason and Joe Vaneck's two visits with *La Cena delle Beffe* (Giordano) in 1987, introducing a remarkable young American soprano, Alessandra Marc, in a minor role, and Prokofiev's *The Duenna* (1989), with Neil Jenkins in top form, even playing the musical glasses himself in the finale.

One of Elaine Padmore's innovative ideas was the Opera Scenes. These started in 1982 as a means of providing opera for the local community at economic prices, starting with £1 tickets that year. Over the years these presentations have allowed members of the chorus and those taking smaller roles to be heard singing more significant parts. The Scenes have become an integral part of the Festival and were further developed by Luigi Ferrari in 1997, when he introduced "mini-operas": condensed version of the mainstream repertory staged in the same style, using limited costumes and sets, with piano accompaniment. Many subsequently well-known names have had early exposure to operatic audiences through the Scenes and Mini-operas over the last two decades.

Scene from Donizetti's *L'Assedio di Calais* 1991

Neil Jenkins as Don Jerome rehearses his group of musicians in
Prokofiev's *The Duenna* 1989.

In 1987 the second major overhaul of the Theatre was undertaken, though without having to miss a season as happened in 1960. The then President of Ireland, Dr Patrick J. Hillery, re-opened the building on September 5th, ahead of the Festival, with a Gala Concert featuring soprano Daniela Bechly, who had appeared as the Goose Girl in Humperdinck's *Königskinder* at the previous Festival, accompanied by John O'Conor. In his address the President commented: "What has been achieved here is the admirable result of a spirit of confidence which puts to shame the plague of pessimism which seems at times to be about to rob us of the will to action". The President's accolade continues to be reflected in the dynamic way the Festival has grown in the intervening years. The new foyer provided a more glamorous entrance to the Theatre, extra rows of seats were cantilevered out over the back of the balcony and many back-stage improvements were undertaken.

In the late 1980's the Festival appointed its first fulltime Chief Executive Jerome Hynes who had previously served as General Manager with the Druid Theatre in Galway. This successful marriage of professionalism and the voluntary was to prove an important factor in the continued development of the Festival in subsequent years. The Festival itself was subsequently extended twice – in 1989 and 1991 – and now runs to a full eighteen days; these extensions to the Theatre and the longer duration, led to a doubling of capacity in the late 1980s and early 1990s. In 1993 additional property was secured and a major re-modelling of the foyers took place. The development of the Festival financially, administratively and in terms of its home, the Theatre Royal, continues today.

In 1988 the recitals included a concert by the first winner of the GPA Dublin International Piano Competition, Philippe Cassard, and led to a series of visits from winners of this tri-ennial Competition over subsequent years. It was also the first time winners of the prestigious Belvedere Competition, Vienna, (the International Hans-Gabor-Belvedere Singing Competition as it is now known in honour of its founder) sang at a Wexford concert. In 1989 a special "Young Ireland" concert introduced examples of the rapidly expanding group of outstanding Irish singers, in a recital by leading young artists featuring Regina Nathan, soprano, Oonagh Keogh, violin, Neil Cooney, piano and Mary Collins, piano.

The Wexford School of Music was also developing into an important musical force. Started

Anatoly Lochak in Tchaikovsky's *Cherevichki* 1993.

in 1980 by former Festival chorus master Alan Cutts (1976-1979), the School contributed a number of important performances over these years. Scottish Opera's Education Unit also visited the Festival, bringing exciting projects to the schools of Wexford between 1987 and 1990.

In 1989, following the death of the Festival's founding director, Dr Tom Walsh, the previous November, the Festival inaugurated the Dr. Tom Walsh Memorial Lectures, initiated by the then Editor of Opera Magazine, Rodney Milnes. These have continued annually, bringing many famous names back to Wexford to reflect on a wide range of Festival and general operatic issues. To date lectures have been given by Ronald Crichton, Derek Hill, Elaine Padmore, Francesca Zambello, Julian Budden, Jan Smaczny, Geoffrey Norris, Ugo Benelli, Graziella Sciutti and Peter Ebert.

• • •

By 1990 the Festival programme had expanded into presenting some 34 musical events, not counting the many exhibitions, plays, traditional music and other concerts featured in the Fringe. Contemporary Irish opera was heard again in 1991 when Opera Theatre Company brought its production of four one-act operas to the Festival, three written by Irish composers John Buckley, Raymond Deane, Marion Ingolsby and one by English composer, Kenneth Chalmers. A first visit from the Ulster Orchestra and the Belfast Philharmonic Society Choir also graced 1991 with a memorable performance of Elgar's *The Dream of Gerontius* under John Lubbock.

In 1990 another concert of successful artists from the Belvedere Competition was staged, including a young winner: Angela Gheorghiu. Other artists to visit Wexford during these years included Jorma Hynninen, Rosemary Ashe, the Vogler Quartet, the Fairer Sax, Torleif Thedeen, Leslie Howard, La Grand Sceana New York, George Melly, Yvonne Kenny, Opera Circus and the Moscow Piano Trio. One remarkable example of intuitive casting can be seen in the 1991 Opera Scenes when Ms. Padmore included four young Irish singers: Majella Cullagh, Lynda Lee, Cara O'Sullivan and Nicola Sharkey, all of whom have made distinguished careers for themselves subsequently. In 1993 pianist John O'Conor returned to the Festival to mark his silver jubilee as a performer in a special recital. Elaine Padmore's last season took place in 1994, she then departed for the Royal Opera in Copenhagen, and more recently has joined the Royal

1999 *Straszny Dwór* by Stanislaw Moniuszko.
Iwona Hossa as Hanna, Viktoria Vizin as Jadwiga.

Opera, Covent Garden, as Head of Opera. It included a visit from the European Community Chamber Orchestra, and recitals by Alison Browner and the latest GPA Dublin International Piano Competition winner, Davide Franceschetti.

She was succeeded by the Director of the Rossini Festival in Pesaro, Luigi Ferrari, who was more recently appointed Director of the prestigious Teatro Comunale di Bologna. This brought a further change of style and direction, introducing a strong emphasis on the Italian and late Romantic repertory, including Meyerbeer's *L'Étoile du Nord* (1996), with Juan Diego Flórez in the cast, and the first Western European performance of *Sarlatán* (1998) by Pavel Haas, a Czech composer lost in the Holocaust. The Festival's first Polish opera *The Haunted Manor* (Moniuszko's *Straszny dwór*) was seen in 1999. During his directorship, Luigi Ferrari has added many personal touches. The development of the mini-opera has already been noted, he also introduced the Prague Chamber Choir, who sing in the opera chorus and give recitals on their own, as a regular feature of the Festival's programme in recent years. He has also developed the series of lunch-time concerts by Festival artists, as well as themed concerts related to that year's opera programme. Significant artists who have appeared during Ferrari's period at the Festival include Anatoly Lochak, Vladimir Matorin, Alexandrina Pendatchanska, Elizabeth Futral, Juan Diego Flórez, Svetelina Vassileva, Alexander Safina, Louise Walsh, Joseph Calleja, Iwona Hossa, Elisabeth Woods, Ermonolena Jaho and Tatiana Monogarova. Conductors have included Alexander Anissimov, Vladimir Jurowski, Bruno Aprea, Maurizio Benini, Israel Yinon, Daniele Callegari, David Jones and Alexander Voloschuk.

In 1994 Rubenstein's *The Demon* started a valuable four-year series of commercial recordings from the Festival on the Marco Polo label, one opera per season. It was followed by *Saffo* (Pacini – 1995). *L'Étoile du Nord* (Meyerbeer – 1996) and *Elena da Feltre* (Mercadante – 1997). A new series of Festival CDs will start this year, produced by the Italian label, Fonè, issuing all three operas starting with the three productions from 2001. Radio Telefís Éireann has broadcast the Festival productions right from the start, with Norris Davidson presenting the first and subsequent seasons, a position he fulfilled with wit and charm for over 40 years, with RTÉ's Lyric FM station with Ray Lynott presenting, taking over in recent years. Many seasons have also been relayed by the BBC with Sean Rafferty presenting on BBC Radio 3 in recent years.

The Radio Éireann Light Orchestra played for the first decade of the Festival and was succeeded for one year by the Liverpool Philharmonic and then, in 1962 by the Radio Telefís Éireann Symphony Orchestra, which was expanded in 1989 and re-named the National Symphony Orchestra of Ireland. In 2001, however, due to contractual problems, the Orchestra was replaced for the time-being at least by the National Philharmonic Orchestra of Belarus.

By the mid 1990s the Festival was achieving a consistent 100% occupancy, probably unique in these islands, so it was hardly surprising that thoughts again turned to development. Unanimous in its belief that this was both possible and necessary, the Board considered several options, including an extension to twenty-four days and a fresh start on a greenfield site at the edge of the town, before choosing to pursue a major expansion on the existing site. In pursuit of this a number of properties on High Street have been purchased and, most importantly, in 1999 the Festival's long-standing neighbours, the People Newspapers, were persuaded to relocate and to sell their 11,000 square-feet site to the Festival. These purchases have meant a significant increase to the Theatre's footprint, allowing for major developments to be planned.

The feasibility study has been completed, a private Foundation has been established and, critically, the Government, through An Taoiseach, Mr. Bertie Ahern TD, has committed itself to the project. It is an ambitious scheme, leading to state-of-the-art facilities. Seating will expand from 550 to 750, a second theatre and an art gallery will be added, valuable not just during the Festival but throughout the year, and providing a major centre for the arts. For over fifty years the Festival has been ambitious and it enters its new half-century with confidence. Its financial survival has come through a healthy mixture of Arts Council funding, commercial sponsorship, with Guinness as Principal Sponsor for over three decades, and through its box-office earnings. Each year brings new challenges but Wexford has become adept at dealing with these without indulging in any complacency.

With the experience of 136 operas to date the Festival has built up a remarkable data-bank of knowledge in many diverse areas. The Festival's dedicated but tiny staff could never cope with its gigantic programme without the hugely loyal team of voluntary workers working back stage and front-of-house, and undertaking many other functions at each Festival. The Festival Board, has been led by a distinguished group of Chairmen from Dr Tom through Fr M.J. O Neill, Sir Alfred Beit, Dr J D Ffrench, Sean Scallan, Brig. Richard Jefferies, Jim Golden, Barbara Wallace and John O'Connor to the present incumbent Ted Howlin, all dedicated in their commitment. In addition there has been a long list of Council and Board members who have worked tirelessly for the Festival over the years.

The true spirit of Wexford, however, as Sir Compton Mackenzie and President Hillery rightly identified many years ago, comes from the people of Wexford; it is they who make it great and without whom it simply could not exist.

IAN FOX

Ian Fox is a music lecturer and broadcaster. He is Music Critic of the Sunday Tribune, Irish correspondent to Opera Magazine and a frequent contributor to Lyric FM, RTÉ's classical music channel. He is a member of the Critics' Circle, London and a Council Member of Wexford Festival Opera

THE FIFTIETH WEXFORD FESTIVAL *Alessandro Stradella* by Fredrich Flotow. Declan Kelly as Barbarino, Frantisek Zahradnicek as Malvolio, Ekaterina Morozova as Leonore, Stefano Costa as Alessandro Stradella.

THE FIFTIETH WEXFORD FESTIVAL *Jakobín* by Antonín Dvořák
Tatjana Monogarova as Julie, Markus Werba as Bohus

THE FIFTIETH WEXFORD FESTIVAL *Sapho* by Jules Massenet.
Giuseppina Piunti as Fanny Legrand, Brandon Jovanovich as Jean Gaussin

Artists & repertoire 1951 – 2001

■ 1951

The Rose of Castile *Michael William Balfe*
1, 2, 3, 4 November

Queen Elvira of Leon	MAUREEN SPRINGER
Donna Carmen	ANGELA O'CONNOR
The Duchess of Calatrava	STATIA KEYES
Don Pedro	JAMES G CUTHBERT
Don Florio	JAMES BROWNE
Don Sallust	MICHEL HANLON
Louisa	NELLIE WALSH
Pablo	SEAMUS ROCHE
Don Alvaro	BRENDAN NOLAN
Manuel	MURRAY DICKIE

Wexford Festival Chorus
Chorus Coach MRS N J HORE

Radio Éireann Light Orchestra
Conductor DERMOT O'HARA

Director POWELL LLOYD
Prima Ballerina JOAN DENISE MORIARTY

■ 1952

L'Elisir D'Amore *Gaetano Donizetti*
29, 30 October, 1, 2 November

Adina	ELVINA RAMELLA
Nemorino	NICOLA MONTI
Belcore	GINO VANELLI
Dulcamara	DALLAMANGAS
Gianetta	PATRICIA O'KEEFFE

Wexford Festival Chorus
Chorus Coach MRS N J HORE

Radio Éireann Light Orchestra
Conductor DERMOT O'HARA

Director PETER EBERT
Designer JOSEPH CARL

■ 1953

Don Pasquale *Gaetano Donizetti*
28, 29, 31, October, 1 November

Don Pasquale	CRISTIANO DALLAMANGAS
Ernesto	NICOLA MONTI
Dr Malatesta	AFRO POLI
Norina	ELVINA RAMELLA

Wexford Festival Chorus
Chorus Coach MRS N J HORE

Radio Éireann Light Orchestra
Conductor BRYAN BALKWILL

Director PETER EBERT
Designer JOSEPH CARL

■ 1954

La Sonnambula *Vincenzo Bellini*
3, 4, 6, 7 November

Amina	MARILYN COTLOW
Elvino	NICOLA MONTI
Rudolpho	FRANCO CALABRESE
Teresa	THETIS BLACKER
Lisa	HALINKA DE TARCZYNSKA
Alessio	GWYN GRIFFITHS
A Notary	DANIEL McCOSHAN

Wexford Festival Chorus
Chorus Coach MRS N J HORE
Assistant Chorus Coach NORA O'LEARY

Radio Éireann Light Orchestra
Conductor BRYAN BALKWILL

Director PETER EBERT
Designer JOSEPH CARL

■ *1955*

Manon Lescaut *Giacomo Puccini*
30 October, 1, 3, 5 November

Edmondo	KEVIN MILLER
Chevalier des Grieux	SALVATORE PUMA
Lescaut	MARKO ROTHMÜLLER
Geronte de Ravoir	GWYN GRIFFITHS
Manon Lescaut	ESTHER RÉTHY
Innkeeper	GEOFFREY CLIFTON
Dancing Master	DANIEL MCCOSHAN
Sergeant of the Royal Archers	GEOFFREY CLIFTON
Lamplighter	DANIEL MCCOSHAN
A Singer	CELINE MURPHY

Wexford Festival Chorus
Chorus Coach	MRS N J HORE
Assistant Chorus Coach	NORA O'LEARY

Radio Éireann Light Orchestra
Conductor	BRYAN BALKWILL
Director	ANTHONY BESCH
Designer	PETER RICE

■ *1955*

Der Wildschütz *Albert Lortzing*
31 October, 2, 4, 6 November

Count of Eberbach	THOMAS HEMSLEY
The Countess	MONICA SINCLAIR
Baron Kronthal	JOHN KENTISH
Baroness Freimann	ELIZABETH
LINDERMEIER	
Nanette	CELINE MURPHY
Baculus	MAX PRÖBSTL
Gretchen	HEATHER HARPER
Pancratius	RICHARD DAY

Wexford Festival Chorus
Chorus Coach	MRS C HORE
Assistant Chorus Coach	NORA O'LEARY

Radio Éireann Light Orchestra
Conductor	HANS GIERSTER
Director	ANTHONY BESCH
Designer	PETER RICE

■ *1956*

Martha *Friedrich Von Flotow*
28, 30 October, 1, 3 November

Lady Harriet	GISELA VIVARELLI
Nancy	CONTANCE SHACKLOCK
Sir Tristram Mickleford	GWYN GRIFFITHS
Plunkett	MARKO ROTHMÜLLER
Lionel	JOSEF TRAXEL
The Sheriff of Richmond	GEOFFREY CLIFTON

Wexford Festival Chorus
Chorus Coach	MRS C HORE
Assistant Chorus Coach	NORA O'LEARY

Radio Éireann Light Orchestra
Conductor	BRYAN BALKWILL
Director	PETER POTTER
Designer	JOSEPH CARL

■ *1956*

La Cenerentola *Gioachino Rossini*
29, 31 October, 2, 4 November

Don Ramiro	NICOLA MONTI
Dandini	PAOLO PEDANI
Don Magnifico	CRISTIANO
	DALLAMANGAS
Clorinda	APRIL CANTELO
Thisbe	PATRICIA KERN
Angelina (Cenerentola)	BARBARA HOWITT
Alidoro	JOHN HOLMES

Wexford Festival Chorus
Chorus Coach	MRS C HORE
Assistant Chorus Coach	NORA O'LEARY

Radio Éireann Light Orchestra
Conductor	BRYAN BALKWILL
Director	PETER EBERT
Designer	JOSEPH CARL

■ *1957*

La Figlia Del Reggimento *Gaetano Donizetti*
27, 29, 31 October, 2 November

The Countess of Berkenfeld	PATRICIA KERN
Ortensio	GWYN GRIFFITHS
Sulpizio	GERAINT EVANS
Maria	GRAZIELLA SCIUTTI
Tonio	MARIO SPINA

Wexford Festival Chorus
Chorus Coach	MRS C HORE
Assistant Chorus Coach	NORA O'LEARY

Radio Éireann Light Orchestra
Conductor	BRYAN BALKWILL
Director	PETER EBERT
Designer	JOSEPH CARL

■ 1957

L'Italiana in Algeri *Gioachino Rossini*
28, 30 October, 1, 3 November

Mustafa	PAOLO MONTARSOLO
Elvira	APRIL CANTELO
Zulma	PATRICIA KERN
Haly	GWYN GRIFFITHS
Lindoro	PETRE MUNTEANU
Isabella	BARBARA HOWITT
Taddeo	PAOLO PEDANI

Wexford Festival Chorus
Chorus Coach	MRS C HORE
Assistant Chorus Coach	NORA O'LEARY

Radio Éireann Light Orchestra
Conductor	BRYAN BALKWILL
Director	PETER EBERT
Designer	JOSEPH CARL

■ 1958

I Due Foscari *Giuseppe Verdi*
26, 28, 30 October, 1 November

Francesco Foscari	PAOLO PEDANI
Jacopo Foscari	CARLO DEL MONTE
Lucrezia Contarini	MARIELLA ANGIOLETTI
Jacopo Loredano	PLINIO CLABASSI
Barbarigo	PHILIP TALFRYN
Pisana	ELLEN DALES

Wexford Festival Chorus
Chorus Coach	MRS C HORE
Assistant Chorus Coach	NORA O'LEARY

Radio Éireann Light Orchestra
Conductor	BRYAN BALKWILL
Director	FRANS BOERLAGE
Designer	MICHAEL EVE

■ 1958

Anna Bolena *Gaetano Donizetti*
27, 29, 31 October, 2 November

Henry VIII	PLINIO CLABASSI
Anne Boleyn	MARINA CUCCHIO
Jane Seymour	FIORENZA COSSOTTO
Lord Rochefort	GEOFFREY CLIFTON
Lord Richard Percy	GIANNA JAIA
Smeton	PATRICIA KERN
Sir Hervey	PHILIP TALFRYN

Wexford Festival Chorus
Chorus Coach	MRS C HORE
Assistant Chorus Coach	NORA O'LEARY

Radio Éireann Light Orchestra
Conductor	CHARLES MACKERRAS
Director	PETER POTTER
Designer	MICHAEL EVE

■ 1959

Aroldo *Giuseppe Verdi*
25, 27, 29, 31 October

Aroldo	NICOLA NICOLOV
Mina	MARIELLA ANGIOLETTI
Egberto	ALDO PROTTI
Briano	TREVOR ANTHONY
Godvino	JOHN DOBSON
Enrico	GRIFFITH LEWIS
Elena	ELIZABETH BAINBRIDGE

Wexford Festival Chorus
Chorus Coach	MRS C HORE
Assistant Chorus Coach	NORA O'LEARY

Radio Éireann Light Orchestra
Conductor	CHARLES MACKERRAS
Director	FRANS BOERLAGE
Designer	MICHEÁL MC LIAMMÓIR

■ 1959

La Gazza Ladra *Gioachino Rossini*
26, 28, 30 October, 1 November

Fabrizio Vingradito	TREVOR ANTHONY
Lucia	ELIZABETH BAINBRIDGE
Giannetto	NICOLA MONTI
Ninetta	MARIELLA ADANI
Fernando Villabella	PAOLO PEDANI
Gottardo	GIORGIO TADEO
Pippo	JANET BAKER
Isacco	GRIFFITH LEWIS
Antonio	JULIAN MOYLE
Gregorio	DENNIS WICKS

Wexford Festival Chorus
Chorus Coach	MRS C HORE
Assistant Chorus Coach	NORA O'LEARY

Radio Éireann Light Orchestra
Conductor	JOHN PRITCHARD
Director	PETER POTTER
Designer	OSBERT LANCASTER

■ *1960*

Theatre closed for reconstruction.

■ *1961*

Ernani *Giuseppe Verdi*
24, 26, 28, 30 September

Ernani (John of Aragon)	RAGNAR ULFUNG
Elvira	MARIELLA ANGIOLETTI
Don Carlos	LINO PUGLISI
Don Ruy Gomez	UGO TRAMA
Don Riccardo	CONNALL BYRNE
Jago	JOHN EVANS
Giovanna	ELIZABETH RUST

Wexford Festival Chorus
Chorus Coach — MRS C HORE
Assistant Chorus Coach — NORA O'LEARY

Royal Liverpool Philharmonic Orchestra
Conductor — BRYAN BALKWILL

Director — PETER EBERT
Designer — REGINALD WOOLLEY

■ *1961*

Mireille *Charles Gounod*
25, 27, 29 September, 1 October

Mireille	ANDREA GUIOT
Vincent	ALAIN VANZO
Taven	JOHANNA PETERS
Ourrias	JEAN BORTHAYRE
Vincenette	ELIZABETH RUST
Ramon	FRANCO VENTRIGLIA
Clemence	MORAG NOBLE
Ambroise	DENNIS WICKS
Andreloun	LAURA SARTI

Wexford Festival Chorus
Chorus Coach — MRS C HORE
Assistant Chorus Coach — NORA O'LEARY

Royal Liverpool Philharmonic Orchestra
Conductor — MICHAEL MOORES

Director — ANTHONY BESCH
Designer — OSBERT LANCASTER

■ *1962*

L'Amico Fritz *Pietro Mascagni*
21, 23, 25, 27 October

Fritz Kobus	NICOLA MONTI
Suzel	VERONICA DUNNE
Beppe	BERNADETTE GREEVY
David	PAOLO PEDANI
Hanezo	DERICK DAVIES
Federico	ADRIAN DE PEYER
Caterina	LAURA SARTI

Wexford Festival Chorus
Visiting Chorus Coach — MYER FREDMAN
Wexford Chorus Coach — MRS C HORE
Assistant Chorus Coach — NORA O'LEARY
Assistant Chours Coach — REV FR HUMILIS O.F.M.

Radio Éireann Symphony Orchestra
Conductor — ANTONIO TONINI
Director — MICHAEL HADJI MISCHEV

Designer — REGINALD WOOLLEY

■ *1962*

I Puritani *Vincenzo Bellini*
22, 24, 26, 28 October

Sir Bruno Robertson	ADRIAN DE PEYER
Elvira	MIRELLA FRENI
Lord Arthur Talbot	LUCIANO SALDARI
Sir George Walton	FRANCO VENTRIGLIA
Sir Richard Forth	LINO PUGLISI
Lord Walton	DERICK DAVIES
Queen Henrietta of France	LAURA SARTI

Wexford Festival Chorus
Visiting Chorus Coach — MYER FREDMAN
Wexford Chorus Coach — MRS C HORE
Assistant Chorus Coach — NORA O'LEARY
Assistant Chorus Coach — REV FR HUMILIS O.F.M.

Radio Éireann Symphony Orchestra
Conductor — GUNNAR STAERN

Director — PETER EBERT
Designer — REGINALD WOOLLEY

■ *1963*

Don Pasquale *Gaetano Donizetti*
20, 22, 24, 26 October

Don Pasquale	GUUS HOEKMAN
Dr Malatesta	DINO MANTOVANI
Ernesto	ALFONZ BARTHA
Norina	MARGHERITA RINALDI

Wexford Festival Chorus
Visiting Chorus Coach — Myer Fredman
Wexford Chorus Coach — Mrs C Hore
Assistant Chorus Coach — Nora O'Leary

Radio Éireann Symphony Orchestra
Conductor — Antonio De Almeida

Director — Michael Hadji Mischev
Designer — Anna Hadji Mischev

■ 1963

La Gioconda *Amilcare Ponchielli*
21, 23, 25, 27 October

Barnaba — Lino Puglisi
La Gioconda — Enriqueta Tarrés
La Cieca — Anna Reynolds
Zuàne — Derick Davies
Isèpo — Adrian de Peyer
Enzo Grimaldo — Giuseppe Gismondo
Alvise Badoero — Franco Ventriglia
Laura — Gloria Lane

Wexford Festival Chorus
Visiting Chorus Coach — Myer Fredman
Wexford Chorus Coach — Mrs C Hore
Assistant Chorus Coach — Nora O'Leary

Radio Éireann Symphony Orchestra
Conductor — Gunnar Staern

Director — Peter Ebert
Designer — Reginald Woolley

■ 1963

The Siege of Rochelle *Michael William Balfe*
27 October

Clara — Patricia McCarry
Captain Montalban — Martin Dempsey
Marquis de Valmour — Adrian de Peyer
Count Rosenberg — Brendan McNally
Michel — Derick Davies
Marcella — Anna Reynolds
The Father Guardian — Franco Ventriglia
First Peasant Girl — Angela Jenkins
Second Peasant Girl — Dorothy Wilson

Wexford Festival Chorus
Visiting Chorus Coach — Myer Fredman
Wexford Chorus Coach — Mrs C Hore
Assistant Chorus Coach — Nora O'Leary
Pianist — Jeanie Reddin
Pianist — Courtney Kenny

Director — Douglas Craig
Designer — Reginald Woolley

■ 1964

Lucia di Lammermoor *Gaetano Donizetti*
24, 26, 29, 31 October

Lord Enrico Ashton of Lammermoor — Lino Puglisi
Lucia Ashton — Karola Agai
Sir Edgardo of Ravenswood — Giacomo Aragall
Raimondo Bidebent — Franco Ventriglia
Alisa — Laura Sarti
Lord Arturo Bucklaw — Alastair Newlands
Normanno — Edmund Bohan

Wexford Festival Chorus
Visiting Chorus Coach — Kenneth Montgomery
Wexford Chorus Coach — Mrs C Hore
Assistant Chorus Coach — Nora O'Leary

Radio Éireann Symphony Orchestra
Conductor — Antonio De Almeida

Director — Michel Crochot
Designer — Reginald Woolley

■ 1964

Il Conte Ory *Gioachino Rossini*
25, 27, 30 October, 1 November

Il Conte Ory — Pietro Bottazzo
L'Ajo — Federico Davia
Isoliero — Stefania Malagù
Roberto — Walter Alberti
Un Cavaliere — David Johnston
La Contessa Adele of Formautiers — Alberta Valentini
Formoutiers — Alberta Valentini
Ragonda — Laura Sarti
Alice — Deirdre Pleydell

Wexford Festival Chorus
Visiting Chorus Coach — Kenneth Montgomery
Wexford Chorus Coach — Mrs C Hore
Assistant Chorus Coach — Nora O'Leary

Radio Éireann Symphony Orchestra
Conductor — Gunnar Staern

Director — Peter Ebert
Designer — Reginald Woolley

■ 1964

Much Ado About Nothing Charles V. Stanford
28 October, 1 November

Hero	ERICA BAX
Beatrice	SOO-BEE LEE
Don Pedro	NOEL NOBLE
Don John	JOHN MACNALLY
Claudio	DENNIS BRANDT
Benedick	RICHARD GOLDING
Leonato	HERBERT MOULTON
Borachio	EDMUND BOHAN
Friar Francis	FRANK OLEGARIO
Dogberry	FRANK OLEGARIO
Seacole	DAVID JOHNSTON
Verges	TONY DALY

Wexford Festival Chorus
Visiting Chorus Coach — KENNETH MONTGOMERY
Wexford Chorus Coach — MRS C HORE
Assistant Chorus Coach — NORA O'LEARY

Radio Éireann Symphony Orchestra
Conductor — COURTNEY KENNY

Director — PETER EBERT
Designer — REGINALD WOOLLEY

■ 1964

Corno di Bassetto
31 October

An entertainment devised by T J Walsh from the musical criticisms of Bernard Shaw.

BERNADETTE GREEVY, FRANCO VENTRIGLIA, JEANNIE REDDIN, JOHN WELSH

■ 1965

Don Quichotte Jules Massenet
23, 25, 28, 30 October

La Belle Dulcinée	IVANA MIXOVA
Don Quichotte	MIROSLAV CANGALOVIC
Sancho	LADKO KOROSEC
Pedro	DEIRDRE PLEYDELL
Garcias	CHRISTINE WILSON
Rodriguez	DAVID JOHNSTON
Juan	MINOO GOLVALA
Ténébrun	MAURICE BOWEN
A Bandit	GIUSEPPE SORBELLO
First Footman	JAMES ARMSTRONG
Second Footman	DERMOD GLOSTER

Wexford Festival Chorus
Visiting Chorus Coach — OLIVER BROOME
Wexford Chorus Coach — MRS C HORE
Assistant Chorus Coach — JAMES GAYNOR
Assistant Chorus Coach — JOE LOWNEY

Radio Éireann Symphony Orchestra
Conductor — ALBERT ROSEN

Director — CARL EBERT
Designer — REGINALD WOOLLEY

■ 1965

La Traviata Giuseppe Verdi
24, 26, 28, 30 October

Violetta Valery	JEANNETTE PILOU
Dr Grenvil	ERICH VIETHEER
Marquis d'Obigny	PATRICK MCGUIGAN
Flora Bervoix	GLORIA JENNINGS
Baron Douphol	RICHARD GOLDING
Gastone de Letorièrs	PHILIP LANGRIDGE
Alfredo Germont	VERIANO LUCHETTI
Annina	ROBIN BELL
Giorgio Germont	OCTAV ENIGARESCU
Giuseppe	DERMOD GLOSTER

Wexford Festival Chorus
Visiting Chorus Coach — OLIVER BROOME
Wexford Chorus Coach — NORA O'LEARY
Assistant Chorus Coach — JAMES GAYNOR
Assitant Chorus Coach — JOE LOWNEY

Radio Éireann Symphony Orchestra
Conductor — GUNNAR STAERN

Director — PETER EBERT
Designer — REGINALD WOOLLEY

■ 1965

La Finta Giardiniera W.A. Mozart
27, 29, 31 October

La Marchesa Violante Onesti	MATTIWILDA DOBBS
Nardo	FEDERICO DAVIÀ
Don Anchise	FRANCIS EGERTON
Arminda	MADDALENA BONIFACCIO
Serpetta	BIRGIT NORDIN
Il Conte Belfiore	UGO BENELLI
Il Cavaliere Ramiro	STEFANIA MALAGÙ

Radio Éireann Symphony Orchestra Players
Conductor — GUNNAR STAERN

Director — PETER EBERT
Designer — JUDITH EBERT

■ 1966

Fra Diavolo *Daniel François Auber*
23, 25, 27, 29 October

Fra Diavolo	UGO BENELLI
Lord Cockburn	ANTONIO BOYER
Lady Pamela	ANNA REYNOLDS
Lorenzo	NIGEL DOUGLAS
Matteo	PASCHAL ALLEN
Zerlina	ALBERTA VALENTINI
Giacomo	ENRICO FISSORE
Beppo	RENATO ERCOLANI

Wexford Festival Chorus
Visitng Chorus Coach	OLIVER BROWNE
Wexford Chorus Coach	MRS C HORE
Assistant Chorus Coach	NORA O'LEARY

Radio Telefís Éireann Symphony Orchestra
Conductor	MYER FREDMAN
Director	DENNIS MAUNDER
Designer	REGINALD WOOLLEY

■ 1966

Lucrezia Borgia *Gaetano Donizetti*
24, 26, 28, 30 October

Don Alfonso	AYHAN BARAN
Lucrezia Borgia	VIRGINIA GORDONI
Gennaro	ANGELO MORI
Maffio Orsini	STEFANIA MALAGÙ
Liverotto	ALAN MORRELL
Gazella	WYNDHAM PARFITT
Petrucci	PATRICK MC GUIGAN
Vitellozzo	BRUCE LOCHTIE
Gubetta	JAMES CHRISTIANSEN
Rustighello	FRANCIS EGERTON
Astolfo	GORDON FARRELL

Wexford Festival Chorus
Visiting Chorus Master	OLIVER BROWNE
Wexford Chorus Master	MRS C HORE
Assistant Chorus Master	NORA O'LEARY

Radio Telefís Éireann Symphony Orchestra
Conductor	ALBERT ROSEN
Director	FRITH BANBURY
Designer	REGINALD WOOLLEY

■ 1967

Otello *Gioachino Rossini*
21, 23, 26, 28 October

Othello	NICOLA TAGGER
Doge	TERENCE SHARPE
Iago	WALTER GULLINO
Rodrigo	PIETRO BOTTAZZO
Lucio	FREDERICK BATEMAN
Elmiro Barberigo	SILVANO PAGLIUCA
Emilia	MARIA CASULA
Desdemona	RENZA JOTTI
Gondolier	FREDERICK BATEMAN

Wexford Festival Chorus
Chorus Master	ANTHONY HOSE

Radio Telefís Éireann Symphony Orchestra
Conductor	ALBERT ROSEN
Director	ANTHONY BESCH
Designer	JOHN STODDART

■ 1967

Roméo et Juliette *Charles Gounod*
22, 24, 27, 29 October

Juliette	ZUELIKA SAQUE
Stephano	ANNE PASHLEY
Gertrude	PAMELA BOWDEN
Roméo	JEAN BRAZZI
Tybalt	DENNIS BRANDT
Benvolio	FREDERICK BATEMAN
Mercutio	HENRI GUI
Paris	KENNETH REYNOLDS
Grégorio	TERENCE SHARPE
Capulet	JAROSLAV HORAČEK
Frère Laurent	VICTOR DE NARKÉ
Le Duc de Verone	RICHARD VAN ALLAN

Wexford Festival Chorus
Chorus Master	ANTHONY HOSE

Radio Telefís Éireann Symphony Orchestra
Conductor	DAVID LLOYD-JONES
Director	JOHN COX
Designer	PATRICK MURRAY

■ 1968

La clemenza di Tito *Wolfgang Amadeus Mozart*
25, 28, 31 October, 2 November

Titus	PETER BAILLIE
Vitellia	HANNEKE VAN BORK
Sextus	PARI SAMAR

Annius	DELIA WALLIS
Servilia	ELAINE HOOKER
Publius	SILVANO PAGLIUCA

Wexford Festival Chorus
Chorus Master — GORDON KEMBER

Radio Telefís Éireann Symphony Orchestra
Conductor — THEODOR GUSCHLBAUER

Director — JOHN COPLEY
Designer — MICHAEL WALLER

■ 1968

La Jolie Fille de Perth *Georges Bizet*
26, 30 October, 1, 3 November

Catherine Glover	DENISE DUPLEIX
Mab	ISABEL GARCISANZ
Henri Smith	JOHN WAKEFIELD
Le Duc de Rothesay	HENRI GUI
Ralph	ROGER SOYER
Simon Glover	SILVANO PAGLIUCA
Un Seigneur	MAURICE ARTHUR
Le Majordome	BRIAN DONLAN
Dancer	ALEXANDER ROY
Dancer	CHRISTINA GALLEA

Wexford Festival Chorus
Chorus Master — GORDON KEMBER

Radio Telefís Éireann Symphony Orchestra
Conductor — DAVID LLOYD-JONES

Director — PAULINE GRANT
Designer — ROBIN ARCHER

■ 1968

L'equivoco stravagante *Gioacchino Rossini*
27, 29, 31 October, 2 November

Gamberotto	RICHARD VAN ALLAN
Ernestina	NELIE PRAGANZA
Ermanno	PIETRO BOTTAZZO
Buralicchio	ELFEGO ESPARZA
Frontino	MARIO CARLIN
Rosalia	MARIA CASULA

Wexford Festival Chorus
Chorus Master — GORDON KEMBER

Radio Telefís Éireann Symphony Orchestra
Conductor — ALDO CECCATO

Director — JOHN COX
Designer — JOHN STODDART

■ 1969

L'infedeltà delusa *Joseph Haydn*
24, 26, 30 October, 1 November

Vespina	EUGENIA RATTI
Sandrina	JILL GOMEZ
Filippo	ALEXANDER YOUNG
Nencio	UGO BENELLI
Nanni	EFTIMIOS MICHALOPOULOS

Radio Telefís Éireann Symphony Orchestra
Conductor — DAVID LLOYD-JONES
Harpsichord Continuo — MARK ELDER

Director — JOHN COPLEY
Designer — JOHN FRASER

■ 1969

Luisa Miller *Giuseppe Verdi*
25, 27, 29, 31 October, 2 November

Count Walter	SILVANO PAGLIUCA
Rodolfo	ANGELO LO FORESE
Federica	BERNADETTE GREEVY
Wurm	EFTIMIOS MICHALOPOULOS
Miller	TERENCE SHARPE
Luisa	LUCIA KELSTON
Laura	ENID HARTLE
A Countryman	STEPHEN TUDOR

Wexford Festival Chorus
Chorus Master — HENRY WARD
Chorus Coach — MELANIE CROWTHER
Chorus Coach — PATRICK MURPHY

Radio Telefís Éireann Symphony Orchestra
Conductor — MYER FREDMAN

Director — JOHN COX
Designer — BERNARD CULSHAW

■ 1970 *(Double Bill)*

A) L'Inganno Felice *Gioacchino Rossini*
23, 26, 30 October, 1 November

Isabella	JILL GOMEZ
Bertrando	UGO BENELLI
Ormondo	ROBERT BICKERSTAFF
Batone	FREDERICO DAVIÀ
Tarabotto	ELFEGO ESPARZA

B) Giovedi Grasso Gaetano Donizetti
23, 26, 30 October, 1 November

The Colonel	FEDERICO DAVIÀ
Nina	JILL GOMEZ
Teodoro	MALCOLM WILLIAMS
Sigismondo	ELFEGO ESPARZA
Camilia	JOHANNA PETERS
Stefanina	JANET HUGHES
Ernesto	UGO BENELLI
Cola	BRIAN DONLAN

Radio Telefís Éireann Symphony Orchestra
Conductor	DAVID ATHERTON
Director	PATRICK LIBBY
Designer	JOHN FUZSER

■ 1970

Lakmé Leo Delibes
24, 27, 29, 31 October

Lakmé	CHRISTIANE EDA-PIERRE
Mallika	YVONNE FULLER
Rose	ANGELA WHITTINGHAM
Ellen	CARMEL O'BYRNE
Mistress Bentson	GABRIELLE RISTORI
Gerald	JOHN STEWART
Nilakantha	JACQUES MARS
Frederic	WILLIAM ELVIN
Hagi	MALCOLM WILLIAMS
Dancer	LYN WALKER
Dancer	ANTHONY BREMNER

Wexford Festival Chorus
Chorus Master	KENNETH CLEVELAND
Voice Coach	PATRICK MURPHY
Voice Coach	MELANIE CROWTHER

Radio Telefís Éireann Symphony Orchestra
Conductor	DAVID LLOYD-JONES
Director	MICHAEL HADJIMISCHEV
Designer	JOHN FRASER
Choreographer	OENONE TALBOT

■ 1970

Albert Herring Benjamin Britten
25, 28, 31 October

Lady Billows	MILLA ANDREW
Florence Pike	JOHANNA PETERS
Miss Wordsworth	PATRICIA REAKES
Mr Gedge	JOHN KITCHINER
Mr Upfold	PATRICIA RING
Superintendant Budd	ELFEGO ESPARZA
Sid	ALAN OPIE
Albert Herring	ALEXANDER OLIVER
Nancy	DELIA WALLIS
Mrs Herring	ENID HARTLE
Emmie	LAUREEN LIVINGSTONE
Cis	LILLIAN WATSON
Harry	ROBIN MCWILLIAMS

Ensemble from Radio Telefís Éireann Symphony Orchestra
Conductor	DAVID ATHERTON
Director	MICHAEL GELIOT
Designer	JANE BOND

■ 1971

Les Pêcheurs de Perles Georges Bizet
21, 24, 26, 29 October

Leila	CHRISTIANE EDA-PIERRE
Nadir	JOHN STEWART
Zurga	MARCO BAKKER
Nourabad	JUAN SOUMAGNAS

Wexford Festival Chorus
Chorus Master	KENNETH CLEVELAND
Chorus Coach	MELANIE CROWTHER
Chorus Coach	PATRICK MURPHY

Radio Telefís Éireann Symphony Orchestra
Conductor	GUY BARBIER
Director	MICHAEL GELIOT
Set Designer	ROGER BUTLIN
Costume Designer	JANE BOND
Lighting Designer	ROBERT BRYAN
Choreographer	ANTHONY BREMNER

■ 1971

La Rondine Giacomo Puccini
22, 25, 28, 31 October

Magda	JUNE CARD
Lisette	ANNE-MARIE BLANZAT
Ruggero	BENIAMINO PRIOR
Prunier	ALEXANDER OLIVER
Rambaldo	THOMAS LAWLOR
Perichaud	BRIAN DONLAN
Gobin	HAROLD SHARPLES
Crebillon	GAVIN WALTON
Yvette	SARA DE JAVELIN
Bianca	SUSAN HOWELLS
Suzy	MYRNA MORENO
A Steward	GAVIN WALTON

Wexford Festival Chorus
Chorus Master	KENNETH CLEVELAND
Chorus Coach	MELANIE CROWTHER

Chorus Coach — PATRICK MURPHY

Radio Telefís Éireann Symphony Orchestra
Conductor — MYER FREDMAN

Director — ANTHONY BESCH
Designer — JOHN STODDART

■ 1971

Il re pastore *Wolfgang Amadeus Mozart*
23, 27, 30 October

Aminta — ANNE PASHLEY
Elisa — NORMA BURROWES
Tamiri — ANNE CANT
Agenore — RICHARD BARNARD
Allessandro — EDUARDO VELAZCO

Radio Telefís Éireann Symphony Orchestra
Conductor — KENNETH MONTGOMERY

Director — JOHN COX
Designer — ELISABETH DALTON

■ 1972

Il Pirata *Vincenzo Bellini*
27, 30 October, 2, 5 November

Ernesto — MARCO BAKKER
Imogene — CHRISTIANE EDA-PIERRE
Gualtiero — WILLIAM MACDONALD
Itulbo — NOEL DRENNAN
Goffredo — HUGH RICHARDSON
Adele — MARY SHERIDAN

Wexford Festival Chorus
Chorus Master — PETER ROBINSON
Chorus Coach — MELANIE CROWTHER
Chorus Coach — PETER MURPHY

Radio Telefís Éireann Symphony Orchestra
Conductor — LEONE MAGIERA

Director — MICHAEL GELIOT
Designer — JANE VENABLES
Lighting Designer — ROBERT BYRAN

■ 1972

Oberon *Carl Maria von Weber*
26, 29, 31 October, 3 November

Oberon — JOHN FRYATT
Titania — LOUISE MANSFIELD
Puck — JANET HUGHES
Huon — HEIKKI SIUKOLA
Gerasmin — BRENT ELLIS

Rezia — VIVIAN MARTIN
Fatima — DELIA WALLIS
Baibars — MICHAEL BEAUCHAMP
Haroun — ANDREW PAGE
Hakim — JOHN FLANAGAN
A Mermaid — SUSAN LEES

Wexford Festival Chorus
Chorus Master — PETER ROBISNON
Chorus Coach — MELANIE CROWTHER
Chorus Coach — PETER MURPHY

Radio Telefís Éireann Symphony Orchestra
Conductor — KENNETH MONTGOMERY

Director — ANTHONY BESCH
Designer — ADAM POLLOCK
Lighting Designer — ROBERT BRYAN

■ 1972

Káta Kabanovà *Leoš Janáček*
28 October, 1, 4 November

Savel Prokofjevic Dikoj — JAN KYZLINK
Boris Grigorjev — IVO ZIDEK
Marfa Ignatevna Kabanova (Kabanicha) — SONA CERVENA
Tichon Ivanyc Kabanov — PATRICK RING
Katerina (Kata) — ALEXANDRA HUNT
Vana Kudrjas — DAVID FIELDSEND
Varvara — ELIZABETH CONNELL
Kuligin — CHRISTIAN DU PLESSIS
Glascha — SUSAN LEES
Fekluscha — NELLIE WALSH

Wexford Festival Chorus
Chorus Master — PETER ROBINSON
Chorus Coach — MELANIE CROWTHER
Chorus Coach — PETER MURPHY

Radio Telefís Éireann Symphony Orchestra
Conductor — ALBERT ROSEN

Director — DAVID POUNTNEY
Designer — SUSAN BLANE
Designer — MARIA BJORNSEN
Lighting Designer — ROBERT BRYAN

■ 1973

Ivan Susanin *M.I. Glinka*
25, 28, 31 October, 2 November

Antonida — HORIANA BRANISTEANU
Vanya — RENI PENKOVA
Sobinin — WILLIAM MCDONALD
Ivan Susanin — MATTI SALMINEN
Sigismund — COLIN FAY

Messenger	DENNIS O'NEILL
Russian Warrior	PETER FOREST
Dancer	TESSA JARVIS
Dancer	ANTON ELDER

Wexford Festival Chorus
Chorus Master	GORDON KEMBER
Chorus Coach	MELANIE CROWTHER

Radio Telefís Éireann Symphony Orchestra
Conductor	GUY BARBIER
Director	MICHAEL HADJIMISCHEV
Designer	SUSAN BLANE
Lighting Designer	WILLIAM BRADFORD
Choreographer	TESSA JARVIS

■ 1973

The Gambler *Sergei Prokofiev*
26, 30 October, 3 November

Baboushka	SONA CERVENA
The General	JOSEPH ROULEAU
Pauline	ANNE HOWELLS
Alexei	ARLEY REECE
Blanche	ANNABEL HUNT
Marquis	BERNARD DICKERSON
Mr Astley	RICHARD STILGOE
Nilsky	DENNIS O'NEILL
Potapitch	PETER FOREST

Wexford Festival Chorus
Chorus Master	GORDON KEMBER
Chorus Coach	MELANIE CROWTHER

Radio Telefís Éireann Symphony Orchestra
Conductor	ALBERT ROSEN
Director	DAVID POUNTNEY
Designer	MARIA BJORNSEN
Lighting Designer	WILLIAM BRADFORD

■ 1973

L'ajo nell'imbarazzo *Gaetano Donizetti*
27, 29 October, 1, 4 November

Il Marchese Giulio Antiquati	MANUEL GONZALEZ
Il Marchese Enrico	SUSO MARIATEGUI
Gilda Tallemanni	SILVIA BALEANI
Il Marchese Pippetto	BERNARD DICKERSON
Don Gregorio Cordebone	RICHARD MCKEE
Leonarda	JOHANNA PETERS
Simone	RICHARD STILGOE

Wexford Festival Chorus
Chorus Master	GORDON KEMBER
Chorus Coach	MELANIE CROWTHER

Radio Telefís Éireann Symphony Orchestra
Conductor	KENNETH MONTGOMERY
Director	PATRICK LIBBY
Designer	ADAM POLLOCK
Lighting Designer	WILLIAM BRADFORD

■ 1974

Medea in Corinto *Giovanni Simone Mayr*
23, 25, 29 October, 1 November

Creusa	EIDDWEN HARRHY
Creonte	LIEUWE VISSER
Giasone	ARLEY REECE
Medea	MARGRETA ELKINS
Ismene	JOAN DAVIES
Egeo	WILLIAM MCKINNEY
Tideo	ROBIN LEGGATE
Evandro	ALEXANDER MAGRI

Wexford Festival Chorus
Chorus Master	KENNETH CLEVELAND
Chorus Coach	MELANIE CROWTHER
Chorus Coach	PATRICK MURPHY

Radio Telefís Éireann Symphony Orchestra
Conductor	RODERICK BRYDON
Director	ADRIAN SLACK
Designer	DAVID FIELDING
Lighting Designer	JAMES MCCOSH

■ 1974

Thaïs *Jules Massenet*
24, 27, 31 October, 3 November

Palemon	LIEUWE VISSER
Athanael	THOMAS MCKINNEY
Thaïs	JILL GOMEZ
Le Serviteur	SEÁN MITTEN
Nicias	FRANCIS EGERTON
Crobyle	HELEN MACARTHUR
Myrtale	ANN MURRAY
Albine	RUTH MAHER

Wexford Festival Chorus
Chorus Master	KENNETH CLEVELAND
Chorus Coach	MELANIE CROWTHER
Chorus Coach	PATRICK MURPHY

Radio Telefís Éireann Symphony Orchestra
Conductor	JACQUES DELACÔTE
Director	JEREMY SUTCLIFFE
Designer	JOHN FRASER
Lighting Designer	JAMIE TAYLOR

■ 1974

Der Barbier von Bagdad *Peter Cornelius*
26, 28, 30 October, 2 November

Nureddin	KEVORK BOYACIYAN
Bostana	JOAN DAVIES
Abul Hassan Ali Ebn Bekar	RICHARD MCKEE
Margiana	HELEN MACARTHUR
The Kadi Baba Mustapha	FRANCIS EGERTON
The Kalif	ANTONY RANSOME
Muezzin 1	SEÁN MITTEN
Muezzin II	MICHAEL SCOTT
Muezzin III	HARRY NICOLL
A Slave	ALEXANDER MAGRI

Wexford Festival Chorus
Chorus Master	KENNETH CLEVELAND
Chorus Coach	MELANIE CROWTHER
Chorus Coach	PATRICK MURPHY

Radio Telefís Éireann Symphony Orchestra
Conductor	ALBERT ROSEN
Director	WOLF SIEGFRIED WAGNER
Set Designer	DACRE PUNT
Costume Designer	ALEX REID
Lighting Designer	JAMIE TAYLOR

■ 1975

Le Roi d'Ys *Edouard Lalo*
23, 26, 29, 31 October

Jahel	MICHEL VALLAT
Rozenn	CHRISTIANE CHATEAU
Margared	GILLIAN KNIGHT
Karnac	STUART HARLING
Mylio	ANTONIO BARASORDA
Le Roi	JUAN SOUMAGNAS
St Corentin	JUAN SOUMAGNAS

Wexford Festival Chorus
Chorus Master	KENNETH CLEVELAND
Chorus Coach	PATRICK MURPHY

Radio Telefís Éireann Symphony Orchestra
Conductor	JEAN PERISSON
Director	JEAN-CLAUDE AUVRAY
Designer	BERNARD ARNOULD
Lighting Designer	JAMES MCCOSH

■ 1975

Eritrea *Francesco Cavalli*
22 (modern première), 25, 28 October, 1 November

Boreas	IAN CADDY
Iris	JESSICA CASH
Alcione	STUART HARLING
Nisa	ANNA BENEDICT
Itidio	JAMES O'NEILL
Eurimidonte	PHILIP LANGRIDGE
Dione	JOHN YORK SKINNER
Laodicea	ANN MURRAY
Misena	JESSICA CASH
Eritrea	ANNE PASHLEY
Theramene	PAUL ESSWOOD
Lesbo	ANNA BENEDICT
Niconida	IAN CADDY
Argeo	MATTEO DE MONTI

Wexford Festival Baroque Ensemble
Conductor	JANE GLOVER
Director	IAN STRASFOGEL
Designer	FRANCO COLAVECCHIA
Lighting Designer	JAMES MCCOSH

■ 1975

La Pietra del Paragone *Gioachino Rossini*
24, 27, 30 October, 2 November

Pacuvio	IAN CADDY
Aspasia	JOAN DAVIES
Fabrizio	JAMES O'NIELL
Donna Fulvia	IRIS DELL'ACQUA
Macrobio	ERIC GARRETT
Giocondo	JOHN SANDOR
Clarice	SANDRA BROWNE
Asdrubale	RICHARD BARRETT

Wexford Festival Chorus
Chorus Master	KENNETH CLEVELAND
Chorus Coach	PATRICK MURPHY

Radio Telefís Éireann Symphony Orchestra
Conductor	RODERICK BRYDON
Director	ADRIAN SLACK
Designer	JOHN BURY

1976

Giovanna d'Arco *Giuseppe Verdi*
20, 23, 26, 29 October

Delil	ALEXANDER MAGRI
Carlo VII	CURTIS RAYAM
Giacomo	LAJOS MILLER
Giovanna	EMIKO MARUYAMA
Talbot	ARNOLD DVORKIN

Wexford Festival Chorus
Chorus Master	ALAN CUTTS
Chorus Coach	PATRICK MURPHY
Chorus Coach	RUTH MILLER

Wexford Festival Children's Choir
Choir Director	SR MARY WALSH
I.B.V.M.	

Radio Telefís Éireann Symphony Orchestra
Conductor	JAMES JUDD
Director	JEREMY SUTCLIFFE
Designer	DAVID FIELDING
Lighting Designer	GRAHAM LARGE

1976

The Merry Wives of Windsor *Otto Nicolai*
21, 24, 27, (concert performance), 28, 31 October

Mistress Ford	CATHERINE WILSON
Mistress Page	ANNE COLLINS
Mr Page	IAN COMBOY
Slender	KEITH JONES
Dr Caius	SEÁN MITTEN
Fenton	MAURICE ARTHUR
Falstaff	MICHAEL LANGDON
Mr Ford	ALAN OPIE
Townsman	PETER O'LEARY
Ann Page	SANDRA DUGDALE

Wexford Festival Chorus
Chorus Master	ALAN CUTTS
Chorus Coach	RUTH MILLER
Chorus Coach	BERNIE MORRIS

Radio Telefís Éireann Symphony Orchestra
Conductor	LEONARD HANCOCK
Director	PATRICK LIBBY
Designer	ADAM POLLOCK
Lighting Designer	GRAHAM LARGE

1976

The Turn of the Screw *Benjamin Britten*
22, 25, 27, 30 October

The Prologue	MAURICE ARTHUR
The Governess	JANE MANNING
Flora	VICTORIA KLASICKI
Miles	JAMES MAGUIRE
Mrs Grose	MARGARET KINGSLEY
Quint	LEE WINSTON
Miss Jessel	ANNE CANT

Wexford Festival Ensemble
Conductor	ALBERT ROSEN
Director	ADRIAN SLACK
Set Designer	DAVID FIELDING
Lighting Designer	JAMES MCCOSH

1977

Hérodiade *Jules Massenet*
19, 22, (24 October concert performance in Dun Mhuire Hall) 25, 28 October

Phanuel	ALVARO MALTA
Salomé	EILENE HANNAN
Hérode	MALCOLM DONNELLY
Jean (John the Baptist)	JEAN DUPOUY
La Jeune Babylonienne - soprano	HILARY STRAW
Le Jeune Babylonienne - dancer	CLAIR SYMONDS
Hérodiade	BERNADETTE GREEVY
Une Voix	BONAVENTURA BOTTONE
Grand Prêtre	GLYN DAVENPORT
Vitellius	MICHAEL LEWIS

Wexford Festival Chorus
Chorus Master	ALAN CUTTS
Chorus Coach	BERNIE MORRIS
Chorus Coach	RUTH MILLER

Wexford Children's Choir
Choir Coach	SR MARY WALSH I.B.V.M

Radio Telefís Éireann Symphony Orchestra
Conductor	HENRI GALLOIS
Director	JULIAN HOPE
Designer	ROGER BUTLIN
Lighting Designer	JOHN B READ
Choreographer	DOMY REITER-SOFFER

■ 1977

Orfeo ed Euridice *Christophe Willibald Gluck*
20, 23, 26, 29 October

Orfeo	KEVIN SMITH
Euridice	JENNIFER SMITH
Amor	ANNA BENEDICT

Wexford Festival Chorus
Chorus Master	ALAN CUTTS
Chorus Coach	BERNIE MORRIS
Chorus Coach	RUTH MILLER

Irish Ballet Company
Artistic Director	JOAN DENISE MORIARTY

Radio Telefís Éireann Symphony Orchestra
Conductor	JANE GLOVER
Director	WOLF SIEGFRIED WAGNER
Choreographer	DOMY REITER-SOFFER
Costume Designer	ALEX REID
Set Designer	DACRE PUNT
Lighting Designer	JAMES MCCOSH

■ 1977 (Triple Bill)

A) Il Maestro di Cappella *Maffeo Zanon, based on music by Cimarosa*
21, 24, 27, 30 October

Il Maestro	SESTO BRUSCANTINI

B) La Serva e L'Ussero *Luigi Ricci*
21, 24, 27, 30 October

Buontempo	SESTO BRUSCANTINI
Marianna	RUTH MAHER
Angelica	CARMEN LAVANI
Roberto	BONAVENTURA BOTTONE
Andrea	MICHAEL LEWIS

C) La Serva Pandrona *Giovanni Pergolesi*
21, 24, 27, 30 October

Serpina	CARMEN LAVANI
Uberto	SESTO BRUSCANTINI
Vespone	ANGELA AGUADE

Wexford Festival Chorus
Chorus Coach	PATRICK MURPHY
Chorus Master	KENNETH CLEVELAND

Radio Telefís Éireann Symphony Orchestra
Conductor	JAMES JUDD
Director	SESTO BRUSCANTINI
Designer	TIM REED
Lighting Designer	JAN SENDOR

■ 1978

Tiefland *Eugene d'Albert*
25, 28, 31 October, 3 November

Nando	BONAVENTURA BOTTONE
Pedro	MAXWELL HARRISON
Pedro	JON ANDREW
Sebastiano	MALCOLM DONNELLY
Marta	MANI MEKLER
Tommaso	ALVARO MALTA
Pepa	CARMEL PATRICK
Antonia	AIDEEN LANE
Rosalia	CAROLINE TATLOW
Moruccio	PAT SHERIDAN
Nuri	DINAH HARRIS

Wexford Festival Chorus
Chorus Master	ALAN CUTTS

Radio Telefís Éireann Symphony Orchestra
Conductor	HENRI GALLOIS
Director	JULIAN HOPE
Designer	ROGER BUTLIN
Lighting Designer	VICTOR LOCKWOOD
Costume Designer	ALISON MEAGHER AND LUKE PASCOE

■ 1978

Il Mondo Della Luna *Joseph Haydn*
26, 29 October, 1, 4 November

Ecclitico	UGO BENELLI
Scholar 1	PETER O'LEARY
Scholar 2	GERARD DELREZ
Scholar 3	GRAHAM TREW
Scholar 4	GREVILLE O'BRIEN
Buonafede	GIANNI SOCCI
Ernesto	ALAN WATT
Cecco	DENNIS O'NEILL
Clarice	ELAINE LINSTEDT
Flaminia	HELEN DIXON
Lisetta	EMILY HASTINGS

Radio Telefís Éireann Symphony Orchestra
Conductor	JAMES JUDD
Director	ADRIAN SLACK
Set Designer	AXEL BARTZ
Costume Designer	TIM REED
Lighting Designer	VICTOR LOCKWOOD
Continuo	COURTNEY KENNY

1978

The Two Widows *Bedřich Smetana*
27, 30 October, 2, 5 November; 3 November (prom performance)

Karolina	ELIZABETH GALE
Aneska	FELICITY PALMER
Mumlal	JOSEPH ROULEAU
Ladislav	ROBERT WHITE
Lidka	DINAH HARRIS
Tonik	BONAVENTURA BOTTONE

Wexford Festival Chorus
Chorus Master — ALAN CUTTS
Radio Telefís Éireann Symphony Orchestra
Conductor — ALBERT ROSEN

Director — DAVID POUNTNEY
Designer — SUE BLANE
Choreographer — TERRY GILBERT
Lighting Designer — VICTOR LOCKWOOD

1979

L'Amore dei Tre Re *Italo Montemezzi*
24, 27, 30 October, 2 November

Archibaldo	ALVARO MALTA
Falminio	BONAVENTURA BOTTONE
Avito	NEIL McKINNON
Fiora	MAGDALENA CONONOVICI
Manfredo	LAJOS MILLER
Handmaiden	COLETTE McGAHON
A Young Girl	MARIE-CLAIRE O'REIRDAN
A Young Man	WILLIAM PUGH
An Old Woman	COLETTE McGAHON

Wexford Festival Chorus
Chorus Master — ALAN CUTTS

Wexford Children's Choir
Choir Master — SR MARY WALSH I.B.V.M

Radio Telefís Éireann Symphony Orchestra
Conductor — PINCHAS STEINBERG

Director — STEWART TROTTER
Designer — DOUGLAS HEAP
Lighting Designer — GRAHAM LARGE

1979

La Vestale *Gasparo Spontini*
25, 28, 31 October, 3 November

Cinna	TERENCE SHARPE
Licinius	ENNIO BUOSO
La Grande Vestale	CLAIRE LIVINGSTONE
Julia	MANI MEKLER
Le Grand Pontife	RODERICK KENNEDY
Un Consul	PAT SHERIDAN

Wexford Festival Chorus
Chorus Master — ALAN CUTTS
Radio Telefís Éireann Symphony Orchestra
Conductor — MATTHIAS BAMERT

Director — JULIAN HOPE
Set Designer — ROGER BUTLIN
Costume Designer — SUE BLANE
Lighting Designer — GRAHAM LARGE

1979

Crispino e la Comare *Luigi and Federico Ricci*
26, 29 October, 1, 4 November

Don Asdrubale di Caparotta	PAT SHERIDAN
Contino del Fiore	BONAVENTURA BOTTONE
Crispino Tacchetto	SESTO BRUSCANTINI
Annetta	LUCIA ALIBERTI
Mirabolano	GIANNI SOCCI
Fabrizio	DAVID BEAVAN
Donna Giusta, La Comare	RUTH MAHER
Bortolo	PETER O'LEARY
A Crier	MARTIN SHOPLAND
Lisetta	COLETTE McGAHON
Crispino's Child	EOIN COLFER
Crispino's Child	DEIRDRE BROGAN
Crispino's Child	KATHERINE MILLER
Crispino's Child	FERGAL COFFEY
Trumpeter	SEAMUS MAHONY
Drummer	JIMMY BUSHER

Wexford Festival Chorus
Chorus Master — ALAN CUTTS
Radio Telefís Éireann Symphony Orchestra
Conductor — JAMES JUDD

Director — SESTO BRUSCANTINI
Designer — TIM REED
Lighting Designer — GRAHAM LARGE
Continuo — COURTNEY KENNY

1980

Edgar *Giacomo Puccini*
22, 25, 28, 31 October

Fidelia	IRIS DELL'ACQUA
Edgar	NICO BOER
Tigrana	MAGDALENA CONONOVICI
Frank	TERENCE SHARPE
Gaultiero	RODERICK KENNEDY

Wexford Festival Chorus
Chorus Master   Kim Mooney

Bride Street Wexford Boys' Choir
Choir Master   Gerard Lawlor
Radio Telefís Éireann Symphony Orchestra
Conductor   Robin Stapleton

Director   Roger Chapman
Set Designer   Douglas Heap
Costume Designer   Jane Law
Lighting Designer   Graham Large

■ 1980

Orlando *G.F. Handel*
23, 26, 29 October, 1 November

Zoroastro	Roderick Kennedy
Orlando	John Angelo Messana
Dorinda	Lesley Garrett
Angelica	Alison Hargan
Medoro	Bernadette Greevy

Radio Telefís Éireann Symphony Orchestra
Conductor   James Judd

Director   Wilfred Judd
Set Designer   Kandis Cook
Costume Designer   Alison Meagher
Lighting Designer   Graham Large

■ 1980

Of Mice and Men *Carlisle Floyd*
24, 27, 30 October, 2 November

Lennie Small	Curtis Rayam
George Milton	Lawrence Cooper
Curley	John Winfield
Candy	Seán Mitten
Curley's Wife	Christine Isley
Slim	Padraig O'Rourke
Carlson	Brendan Cavanagh
Ballad Singer	Paul Arden Griffith

Wexford Festival Chorus
Chorus Master   Kim Mooney

Radio Telefís Éireann Symphony Orchestra
Conductor   John DeMain

Director   Stewart Trotter
Designer   John Cervenka
Designer   Tim Reed
Lighting Designer   Graham Large

■ 1981

I Gioielli Della Madonna *Ermanno Wolf-Ferrari*
21, 24, 27, 30 October

Maliella	Marie Slorach
Gennaro	Angelo Marenzi
Carmela	Nuala Willis
Rafaele	Carlo Desideri
Biaso	Brendan Cavanagh
Totonno	Harry Nicoll
Ciccillo	Philip Creasy
Rocco	Seán Mitten
Stella	Virginia Kerr
Serena	Marian Finn
Concetta	Nicola Sharkey

Wexford Festival Chorus
Chorus Master   Simon Joly

Bride Street Wexford Boys' Choir
Choir Master   Gerard Lawlor

Radio Telefís Éireann Symphony Orchestra
Conductor   Colman Pearce

Director   Graham Vick
Designer   Russell Craig
Lighting Designer   Graham Large

■ 1981

Zaïde *Wolfgang Amadeus Mozart*
22, 25, 28, 31 October

Zaïde	Lesley Garrett
Gomatz	Neil Mackie
Allazim	Ulrik Cold
Sultan Soliman	Curtis Rayam
Osmin	Gordon Sandison

Radio Telefís Éireann Symphony Orchestra
Conductor   Nicholas Cleobury

Director   Timothy Tyrrel
Designer   Dermot Hayes
Lighting Designer   Graham Large

■ 1981

Un Giorno di Regno *Giuseppe Verdi*
23, 26, 29 October, 1 November

Cavaliere Di Belfiore	Donald Maxwell
Barone Di Kelbar	Sesto Bruscantini
Marchese Del Poggio	Lucia Aliberti
Giulietta Di Kelbar	Angela Feeney
Edoardo Di Sanval	Ugo Benelli
Tesoriere La Rocca	Gianni Socci

Conte Ivrea	BRENDAN CAVANAGH
Delmonte	TONY MADDEN

Wexford Festival Chorus
Chorus Master — SIMON JOLY

Radio Telefís Éireann Symphony Orchestra
Conductor — JAMES JUDD

Director — SESTO BRUSCANTINI
Designer — TIM REED
Lighting Designer — GRAHAM LARGE

■ 1982

Sakùntala *Franco Alfano*
20, 23, 26, 29 October

Sakùntala	EVELYN BRUNNER
Durvàsas	RICHARD ROBSON
Harita	BRIAN KEMP
A young hermit	HARRY NICOLL
The King	DAVID PARKER
Anusuya	ROSAMUND ILLING
Priyamvada	ANITA TERZIAN
The Kings Squire	ANDREW GALLACHER
Kanva	ARMANDO CAFORIO
A fisherman	BRENDAN CAVANAGH

Wexford Festival Chorus
Chorus Master — SIMON JOLY
Local Chorus Master — GERARD LAWLOR

Radio Telefís Éireann Symphony Orchestra
Conductor — ALBERT ROSEN
Director — NICHOLAS HYTNER
Designer — DAVID FIELDING
Lighting Designer — MICK HUGHES

■ 1982 (Double Bill)

A) Arianna a Naxos *Haydn*
October 21, 24, 27, 30

Ariadne — BERNADETTE GREEVY

B) L'isola Disabitata *Haydn*
October 21, 24, 27, 30

Costanza, Gernando's wife	BERNADETTE GREEVY
Silvia	URSULA REINHARDT-KISS
Enrico	PHILIP GELLING
Gernando	MALDWYN DAVIES

Radio Telefís Éireann Symphony Orchestra
Conductor — NEWELL JENKINS

Director — GUUS MOSTART
Designer — JOHN OTTO
Lighting Designer — MICK HUGHES
Choreographer — NIGEL NICHOLSON

■ 1982

Grisélidis *Jules Massenet*
22, 25, 28, 31 October

Alain	HOWARD HASKIN
Gondebaut	RICHARD ROBSON
The Prior	CHRISTOPHER BLADES
Marquis de Saluces	SERGEI LEIFERKUS
Grisélidis	ROSEMARIE LANDRY
Bertrade	JOAN MERRIGAN
The Devil	GUNTER VON KANNEN
Fiamina	ROSANNE CREFFIELD

Wexford Festival Chorus
Chorus Master — SIMON JOLY

Radio Telefís Éireann Symphony Orchestra
Conductor — ROBIN STAPLETON

Director — STEPHEN PIMLOTT
Designer — ARIANE GASTAMBIDE
Lighting Designer — MICK HUGHES

■ 1983

Hans Heiling *Heinrich Marschner*
20, 23, 26, 29 October

Hans Heiling	SERGEI LEIFERKUS
The Queen	MALMFRID SAND
Anna	CONSTANCE CLOWARD
Gertrude	INGRID STEGER
Konrad	EDUARDO ALVARES
Stephan	RICHARD LLOYD-MORGAN

Wexford Festival Chorus
Chorus Master — SIMON JOLY
Local Chorus Master — GERARD LAWLOR

Radio Telefís Éireann Symphony Orchestra
Conductor — ALBERT ROSEN

Director — STEPHEN PIMLOTT
Designer — DAVID FIELDING
Lighting Designer — MICK HUGHES
Choreographer — TERRY JOHN BATES

■ 1983

La Vedova Scaltra *Ermanno Wolf-Ferrari*
21, 24, 27, 30 October

Monsieur le Bleau	GRANT SHELLEY
The Conte di Bosco Nero	HOWARD HASKIN
Milord Runebif	NEIL JANSEN
Don Alvaro de Castille	TOM MCDONNELL
Arlecchino	GORDON SANDISON
Rosaura	JILL GOMEZ
Marionette	ROSEMARY ASHE
Folletto	CHRISTOPHER ADAMS
Pedro	ANDREW GALLACHER
Birif	RICHARD LLOYD-MORGAN
Lady	MARILYN HUNT
Lady	SUSAN LEES

Radio Telefís Éireann Symphony Orchestra

Conductor	YAN PASCAL TORTELIER
Director	CHARLES HAMILTON
Designer	TIM REED
Lighting Designer	MICK HUGHES
Choreographer	TERRY JOHN BATES

■ 1983

Linda di Chamounix *Gaetano Donizetti*
22, 25, 28, 31 October

Maddalena	JENNIFER ADAMS
Antonio	BRIAN KEMP
The Marquis di Boisfleury	GIANNI SOCCI
The intendant	BRENDAN CAVANAGH
Linda	LUCIA ALIBERTI
Carlo	UGO BENELLI
The Prefect	JOHN O'FLYNN

Wexford Festival Chorus

Chorus Master	SIMON JOLY
Local Chorus Master	GERARD LAWLOR

Radio Telefís Éireann Symphony Orchestra

Conductor	GABRIELE BELLINI
Director	JULIAN HOPE
Designer	ANNENA STUBBS
Lighting Designer	MICK HUGHES

■ 1984

Le Jongleur De Notre-Dame *Jules Massenet*
24, 27, 30 October, 2 November

Jean (The Juggler)	PATRICK POWER
The Prior	CHRISTIAN DU PLESSIS
Boniface	SERGEI LEIFERKUS
A Musician Monk	JOHN CASHMORE
A Sculptor Monk	RICHARD ROBSON
A painter monk	PETER MCBRIEN
A poet monk	GRANT SHELLEY
A pardoner monk	BRENDAN CAVANAGH
Man in the crowd and offstage voice	RICHARD LLOYD-MORGAN
Angel	VIRGINIA KERR
Angel	ALEXANDRA MERCER
Martin, the jugglers companion	TONY FRIEL

Wexford Festival Chorus

Chorus Master	MARTIN MERRY

Radio Telefís Éireann Symphony Orchestra

Conductor	YAN PASCAL TORTELIER
Director	STEFAN JANSKI
Designer	JOHAN ENGELS
Lighting Designer	MICK HUGHES
Choreographer	TERRY JOHN BATES

■ 1984

Le Astuzie Femminili *Domenico Cimarosa*
25, 28, 31 October, 3 November

Bellina	SUSANNA RIGACCI
Romualdo	PETER-CHRISTOPH RUNGE
Filandro	RAUL GIMENEZ
Giampaolo	ARTURO TESTA
Leonora	NUALA WILLIS
Ersilia	NANCY HERMISTON

Radio Telefís Éireann Symphony Orchestra

Conductor	GYORGY FISCHER
Director	ANDY HINDS
Designer	JOHN MCMURRAY
Lighting Designer	MICK HUGHES
Choreographer	TERRY JOHN BATES
Continuo	COURTNEY KENNY

■ 1984

The Kiss *Bedrich Smetana*
26, 29 October, 1, 4 November

Vendulka	MARIE SLORACH
Paloucký Otec	JOHN AYLDON
Lukáš	EDUARDO ALVARES
Tomeš	ROGER HOWELL
Martinka	PATRICIA JOHNSON
Matouš	RICHARD ROBSON
Barče	NANCY HERMISTON
A Frontier Guard	GRANT SHELLEY

Wexford Festival Chorus
Chorus Master — Martin Merry
Local Chorus Master — Gerard Lawlor

Radio Telefís Éireann Symphony Orchestra
Conductor — Albert Rosen

Director — Toby Robertson
Designer — Bernard Culshaw
Lighting Designer — Mick Hughes
Choreographer — Terry John Bates

■ 1985

La Wally *Alfredo Catalani*
23, 26, 29 October, 1 November

Wally	Josella Ligi
Stromminger	John O'Flynn
Gellner of Hochstoff	Ljubomir Videnov
Hagenbach of Solden	Lawrence Bakst
Walter	Sunny Joy Langton
Afra	Jean Bailey
An old Solider	Richard Robson

Wexford Festival Chorus
Chorus Master — Ian Reid
Local Chorus Master — Gerard Lawlor

Radio Telefís Éireann Symphony Orchestra
Conductor — Albert Rosen

Director — Stefan Janski
Designer — Marie-Jeanne Lecca
Lighting Designer — Mick Hughes
Choreographer — Terry John Bates

■ 1985

Ariodante *George Frideric Handel*
24, 27, 30 October, 2 November

Ariodante	Bernadette Greevy
Ginevra	Pamela Myers
Dalinda	Morag MacKay
Polinesso	Cynthia Clarey
Lurcanio	Raul Gimenez
The King of Scotland	Petteri Salomaa
Odoardo	Adrian Thompson

Irish National Ballet

Wexford Festival Chorus
Chorus Master — Ian Reid
Local Chorus Master — Gerard Lawlor

Radio Telefís Éireann Symphony Orchestra
Conductor — Alan Curtis

Director — Guus Mostart
Designer — John Otto
Lighting Designer — Mick Hughes
Choreographer — Terry John Bates

■ 1985

The Rise and Fall of the City of Mahagonny
Kurt Weill
25, 28, 31 October, 3 November

Leokadja Begbick	Nuala Willis
Trinity Moses	John Gibbs
Fatty the Book-keeper	Valentin Jar
Jenny Smith	Sherry Zannoth
Jimmy Mahoney	Theodore Spencer
Jack	Julian Pike
Bill	Richard Sutcliff
Alaska-Wolf Joe	John O'Flynn
Toby, a witness	Brendan Cavanagh

Members of *Wexford Festival Chorus*
Chorus Master — Ian Reid

Radio Telefís Éireann Symphony Orchestra
Conductor — Simon Joly

Director — Declan Donnellan
Designer — Nick Ormerod
Lighting Designer — Mick Hughes
Choreographer — Terry John Bates

■ 1986

Königskinder *Engelbert Humperdinck*
22, 25, 28, 31 October

Kings Son	William Lewis
Goose-Girl	Daniela Bechly
Witch	Pauline Tinsley
Fiddler	Sergei Leiferkus
Wood-Cutter	Curtis Watson
Broom-Binder	Valentin Jar
Young Girl (wood cutters daughter)	Kathleen Tynan
Inn-Keeper	John O'Flynn
Inn-Keepers Daughter	Roisin McGibbon
Stable Girl	Marijke Hendriks
City Elder	Brian Donlan
Tailor	David Bartleet
Gate-Keeper	Jonathan Veira
Gate-Keeper	Brindley Sherratt

Wexford Festival Chorus
Chorus Master — Ian Reid
Local Chorus Master — Gerard Lawlor

Wexford Children's Chorus
Children's Chorus Master — Gerard Lawlor

Radio Telefís Éireann Symphony Orchestra
Conductor — Albert Rosen

Director — Michael McCaffery
Designer — Di Seymour
Lighting Designer — John Waterhouse
Choreographer — Terry John Bates

■ 1986

Tancredi *Gioacchino Rossini*
23, 26, 29 October, 1 November,
also Queen Elizabeth Hall London 4 November

Tancredi	Kathleen Kuhlmann
Amenaide	Inga Neilsen
Argirio	Bruce Ford
Orbazzano	Petteri Salomaa
Isaura	Marijke Hendriks
Roggiero	Roisin McGibbon

Wexford Festival Male Chorus
Chorus Master — Ian Reid

Radio Telefís Éireann Symphony Orchestra
Conductor — Arnold Oestman

Director — Michael Beauchamp
Designer — William Passmore
Lighting Designer — John Waterhouse

■ 1986

Mignon *Ambroise Thomas*
24, 27, 30 October, 2 November

Mignon	Cynthia Clarey
Wilhelm Meister	Curtis Rayam
Philine	Beverly Hoch
Lothario	Teodor Ciurdea
Laerte	Philip Doghan
Jarno	John O'Flynn
Frédérick	Joseph Cornwell
Antonio	John O'Flynn

Wexford Festival Chorus
Chorus Master — Ian Reid
Local Chorus Master — Gerard Lawlor

Radio Telefís Éireann Symphony Orchestra
Conductor — Yan Pascal Tortelier
Director — Richard Jones
Designer — Richard Hudson
Lighting Designer — John Waterhouse
Choreographer — Terry John Bates

■ 1987

La Straniera *Vincenzo Bellini*
21, 24, 27, 30 October,
also Queen Elizabeth Hall London 3 & 5 November

Alaide	Renata Daltin
Valdeburgo	Jake Gardner
Arturo	Ingus Peterson
Isoletta	Cynthia Clarey
Montolino	Mikhail Krutikov
The Prior	Giancarlo Tosi
Osburgo	Philip Doghan

Wexford Festival Chorus
Chorus Master — Roy Laughlin

Radio Telefís Éireann Symphony Orchestra
Conductor — Jan Latham-Koenig

Director — Robert Carsen
Designer — Russell Craig
Lighting Designer — John Waterhouse
Choreographer — Terry John Bates

■ 1987

La Cena Delle Beffe *Umberto Giordano*
22, 25, 28, 31 October

Tornaquinci	Mikhail Krutikov
Calandra	Oliver Broome
Giannetto Malespini	Fabio Armiliato
Neri Chiaramantesi	Luis Giron May
Gabriello	Philip Doghan
Ginvera	Miriam Gauci
Fazio	David Barrell
Cintia	Kathleen Tynan
Lapo	Bruno Caproni
Doctor	Giancarlo Tosi
Lisabetta	Alessandra Marc
Trinca	Brendan Cavanagh
Fiammetta	Patricia Wright
Laldomine	Kate McCarney
A Singer	Philip Doghan

Radio Telefís Éireann Symphony Orchestra
Conductor — Albert Rosen

Director — Patrick Mason
Designer — Joe Vaněk
Lighting Designer — John Waterhouse

■ 1987

Cendrillon *Jules Massenet*
23, 26, 29 October, 1 November

Pandolfe	Pierre-Yves Le Maigat
Madame de la Haltière	Joan Davies
Noémie	Jane Webster
Dorothée	Therese Feighan
Lucette	Claire Primrose
The Fairy	Silvanna Manga
Prince Charming	Robynne Redmon
The Master of Ceremonies	David Barrell
Dean of the Faculty	Brendan Cavanagh
The First Minister	Patrick Donnelly
The King	Oliver Broome
The Herald	Anthony Morse

Wexford Festival Chorus
Chorus Coach — Roy Laughlin
Local Chorus Master — Gerard Lawlor

Dublin City Ballet

Radio Telefís Éireann Symphony Orchestra
Conductor — Stéphan Cardon

Director — Seamus McGrenera
Designer — Tim Reed
Lighting Designer — John Waterhouse
Choreographer — Terry John Bates

■ 1988

The Devil and Kate Antonin Dvořák
20, 23, 26, 29 October

Jirka — Joseph Evans
Kate — Anne-Marie Owens
Marbuel — Peter Lightfoot
Kate's Mother — Joan Davies
A Musician — Michael Forest
Child — Gavin Clare
Child — Ross Dunphy
Lucifer — Marko Putkonen
Gatekeeper — Phillip Guy-Bromley
Hell Guard — Geoffrey Davidson
Solo Dancer — Julie Wong
The Princess — Kristine Ciesinski
A Chambermaid — Kathleen Tynan
The Marshal — Alan Fairs

Wexford Festival Chorus
Chorus Master — Roy Laughlin
Local Chorus Master — Gerard Lawlor

Radio Telefís Éireann Symphony Orchestra
Conductor — Albert Rosen

Director — Francesca Zambello
Designer — Neil Peter Jampolis
Lighting Designer — Paul Pyant
Choreographer — Terry John Bates

■ 1988

Elisa e Claudio Saverio Mercadante
21, 24, 27, 30 October
also Queen Elizabeth Hall London 3 November

Elisa — Lena Nordin
Claudio — Janos Bandi
Carlotta — Alice Baker
The Conte Arnoldo — Plamen Hidjov
The Marchese Tricotazio — Bruno de Simone
Silvia — Olga Orolinova
Celso — Philip Doghan
Luca — Marko Putkonen
Child — Donal Walsh
Child — Evelyn Walsh

Wexford Festival Chorus
Chorus Master — Roy Laughlin

Radio Telefís Éireann Symphony Orchestra
Conductor — Marco Guidarini

Director & Designer — David Fielding
Co-Designer — Bettina Munzer
Lighting Designer — Paul Pyant

■ 1988 Double Bill

A) Don Giovanni Tenorio Giuseppe Gazzaniga
22, 25, 28, 31 October

Don Giovanni — Miroslav Kopp
Pasquariello — Balazs Poka
The Commendatore — Norman Bailey
Donna Anna — Malmfrid Sand
Donna Elvira — Andrea Bolton
Maturina — Alison Browner
Donna Ximena — Joan Davies
Duke Ottavio — Finbar Wright
Biagio — Alan Cemore
Lanterna — Philip Doghan

B) Turandot Ferruccio Busoni

Kalaf (a prince) — Milan Voldrich
Barak — Balazs Poka
The Emperor Altoum — Norman Bailey
Turandot — Kristine Ciesinski
Adelma — Alison Browner
Truffaldino — Bruce Brewer
Pantalone — Alan Cemore
Tartaglia — Phillip Guy-Bromley
The Queen of Samerkand — Malmfrid Sand
Dancer — Julie Wong
Dancer — Sarah Audsley

Wexford Festival Chorus
Chorus Master — Roy Laughlin

Radio Telefís Éireann Symphony Orchestra
Conductor — Simon Joly

Director — Patrick Mason
Designer — Joe Vaněk
Lighting Designer — Paul Pyant
Choreographer — Terry John Bates

1989

Der Templer Und Die Jüdin *Heinrich Marschner*
26, 29 October, 1, 4, 10 November

Maurice de Bracy	Paul Harrhy
Brian de Bois-Guilbert	William Stone
Rowena	Mary Clarke
Cedric	Bjorn Stockhaus
Wamba	John Daniecki
Oswald	Brian Bannatyne-Scott
Friar Tuck	Adrian Fisher
The Black Knight	Greer Grimsley
Locksley	George Mosley
Rebecca	Anita Soldh
Ivanhoe	Joseph Evans
Isaac of York	William Bankes-Jones
Lucas de Beaumanoir	Peter Loehle

Wexford Festival Chorus
Chorus Master	Jonathan Webb
Local Chorus Master	Gerard Lawlor

Radio Telefís Éireann Symphony Orchestra
Conductor	Albert Rosen
Director	Francesca Zambello
Designer	Bettina Munzer
Lighting Designer	Kevin Sleep

1989

Mitridate, Re de Ponto *Wolfgang Amadeus Mozart*
27, 30 October, 2, 5,
Also Queen Elizabeth Hall 8, 11 November

Mitridate	Martin Thompson
Aspasia	Lena Nordin
Sifare	Cyndia Sieden
Farnace	Luretta Bybee
Ismene	Patricia Rozario
Marzio	Paul Harrhy
Arbate	Therese Feighan

Radio Telefís Éireann Symphony Orchestra
Conductor	Marco Guidarini
Director	Lucy Bailey
Designer	Peter J Davison
Lighting Designer	Kevin Sleep

1989

The Duenna *Sergei Prokofiev*
28, 31 October, 3, 6, 12 November

Don Jerome	Neil Jenkins
Don Issac Mendoza	Spiro Malas
The Duenna	Sheila Nadler
Don Carlos	Thomas Lawlor
Louisa	Amy Burton
Ferdinand	James Busterud
Antonio	Donald George
Clara	Paula Hoffman
Masker 1	Brian Parsons
Masker 2	William Rae
Masker 3	Adrian Fisher
Lopez	Paul Arden-Griffith
Lauretta	Yvonne Brennan
Rosina	Kathleen Tynan
Pedro	Andrew Forbes-Lane
Pablo	Robert Burt
Michael	Garrick Forbes
Father Augustine	Brian Bannatyne-Scott
Brother Elixir	John Daniecki
Brother Chartreuse	Geoffrey Davidson
Brother Benedictine	Björn Stockhaus
Monastery Door Keeper	Ian Baar
Monastery door-keeper	Christopher Speight

Wexford Festival Chorus
Chorus Master	Jonathan Webb

Wexford School of Ballet & Modern Dance

Radio Telefís Éireann Symphony Orchestra
Conductor	František Vajnar
Director	Patrick Mason
Designer	Joe Vaněk
Lighting Designer	Kevin Sleep
Choreographer	Terry John Bates

1990

Zazà *Ruggiero Leoncavallo*
25, 28 October, 1, 4, 9 November

Zazà	Karen Notare
Cascart	John Cimino
Milio Dufresne Pelletier	Claude-Robin
Anaide	Ludmilla Andrew
Natalia	Theresa Hamm
Courtois	Keith Mikelson
Floriana	Yvonne Brennan
Bussy	Wojciech Drabowicz
Duclou	David Cumberland
Michelin	Nigel Leeson-Williams
Augusto	Brendan Cavanagh
Claretta	Constance Novis
Simona	Elizabeth Hetherington
Madame Dufresne	Regina Hanley

Totò Dufresne	Laura Way
Totò Dufresne	Shirley Dempsey
Marco	Nigel Leeson-Williams
A Gentleman	David Buxton
A Gentleman	Mark Pancek

Wexford School of Ballet and Modern Dance

National Symphony Orchestra of Ireland
Conductor	Bruno Rigacci
Director	Jamie Hayes
Designer	Ruari Murchison
Lighting Designer	Mark Pritchard
Choreographer	Terry John Bates

■ 1990

The Rising of the Moon *Nicholas Maw*
26, 30 October, 2, 6, 10 November

Brother Timothy	Francis Egerton
Danal O'Dowd	Gordon Sandison
Cathleen Sweeney	Pamela Helen Stephen
Colonel Lord Jowler	Lawerence Richard
Major Max von Zastrow Runge	Peter-Christoph
Captain Lillywhite	Keith Mikelson
Lady Eugenie Jowler	Pauline Tinsley
Frau Elizabeth von Zastrow	Annika Skoglund
Miss Atalanta Lillywhite	Marie-Claire O'Reirdan
Corporal of Horse Haywood	Max Wittges
Cornet John Stephen Beaumont	Mark Calkins
The Widow Sweeney	Elizabeth Bainbridge
Lynch	Thomas Lawlor
Gaveston	Stephen Crook
Willoughby	David Buxton

Wexford Festival Chorus
Chorus Master	Jonathan Webb

Loch Garman Silver Band

National Symphony Orchestra of Ireland
Conductor	Simon Joly
Director	Ceri Sherlock
Designer	Richard Aylwin
Lighting	Mark Pritchard

■ 1990

La Dame Blanche *François Adrien Boieldieu*
27, 31 October, 3, 7, 11, November

Gabriel	Panaghis Pagoulatos
Dikson	Antoine Normand
Jenny	Brigitte Lafon
Georges Brown	Jorge de Leon
Marguerite	Gillian Knight
Anna	Mariette Kemmer
Gaveston	Andre Cognet
MacIrton	David Cumberland

Wexford Festival Chorus
Chorus Master	Jonathan Webb
Local Chorus Master	Gerard Lawlor

National Symphony Orchestra of Ireland
Conductor	Emmanuel Joel
Director	Jean-Claude Auvray
Designer	Kenny MacLellan
Lighting Designer	Mark Pritchard

■ 1991

L'Assedio di Calais *Gaetano Donizetti*
24, 27, 30 October, 2, 5, 8 November

Eustachio	Victor Ledbetter
Aurelio	Alison Browner
Eleanora	Ann Panagulias
Giovanni d'Aire	Ernesto Grisales
Giacomo de Wisants	Frank Kelley
Pietro de Wisants	Hugh Mackey
Armando	Nigel Leeson-Williams
Edward III	Kurt Ollmann
Isabella	Elizabeth Woollett
Edmondo	Huw Priday
Un Incognito	Andre Cognet
Filippo	Samuel Haythornthwaite
Filippo	Edward Haythornthwaite

Wexford Festival Chorus
Chorus Master	Jonathan Webb

National Symphony Orchestra of Ireland
Conductor	Evelino Pidò
Director	Francesca Zambello
Designer	Alison Chitty
Lighting Designer	Michael Calf

■ 1991

La Rencontre Imprévue *Christoph Willibald Gluck*
25, 28, 31 October, 3, 6, 9 November

Ali	Paul Austin Kelly
Osmin	Christopher Hux
The Calender	Richard Crist
Vertigo	Malcolm Walker
Rezia	Janet Williams

Balkis	KATHRYN COWDRICK
Amine	SANDRA DUGDALE
Dardané	YVONNE BRENNAN
Leader of the Caravan	ANDRE COGNET
The Sultan of Egypt	HUW PRIDAY

Wexford School of Ballet and Modern Dance

National Symphony Orchestra of Ireland
Conductor	RICHARD HICKOX
Director	JAMIE HAYES
Designer	RUARI MURCHISON
Lighting Designer	MICHAEL CALF
Choreographer	GAVIN DORRIAN

■ 1991

Der Widerspenstigen Zähmung *Hermann Goetz*
26, 29 October, 1, 4, 7, 10 November

Baptista	WOLFGANG BABL
Katherina	MARIT SAURAMO
Bianca	ZSUZSANNA CSONKA
Lucentio	STEFAN MARGITA
Hortensio	PETER-CHRISTOPH RUNGE
Petruchio	WILLIAM PARCHER
Grumio	HUGH MACKEY
A Tailor	FRANK KELLEY
Major Domo	HUW RHYS-EVANS
Housekeeper	CARA O'SULLIVAN
Hortensio's wife	JULIE GOSSAGE
Baptista's wife	LYNDA LEE
Katherina's maid	NELLIE WALSH

Wexford Festival Chorus
Chorus Master	JONATHAN WEBB
Local Chorus Master	GERARD LAWLOR

National Symphony Orchestra of Ireland
Conductor	OLIVER VON DOHNANYI
Director/Designer	JOHN LLOYD-DAVIES
Lighting Designer	MICHAEL CALF

■ 1992

Il Piccolo Marat *Pietro Mascagni*
22, 25, 28, 31 October, 3, 6 November

L'Orco	GEORGI SELESNEV
Mariella	KAREN NOTARE
Il Piccolo Marat	THOMAS BOOTH
The Princess de Fleury	PATRICIA MCCAFFREY
Il Soldato	KEITH LATHAM
La Spia	KARL MORGAN DAYMOND
La Tigre	JOSE GARCIA
Il Ladro	JOHANNES VON DUISBURG
Il Carpentiere	RICHARD ZELLER
Captain of the Marats	JOHN RATH
A Bishop	ANDREW HAMMOND
A Prisoner	FAN-CHANG KONG
An Orderly	ROBERT TORDAY
Voice from the crowd	JUSTIN JOSEPH
Voice from the Crowd	NICHOLAS BUXTON
Offstage Tenor voice	KIP WILBORN
Offstage Baritone Voice	GUO YAO YU

Wexford Festival Chorus
Chorus Master	STUART HUTCHINSON

National Symphony Orchestra of Ireland
Conductor	ALBERT ROSEN
Director	STEPHEN MEDCALF
Designer	CHARLES EDWARDS
Lighting Designer	MICHAEL CALF

■ 1992

Gli Equivoci *Stephen Storace*
23, 26, 29, 1, 4, 7 November

Eufemio of Syracuse	KIP WILBORN
Dromio of Syracuse	KURT LINK
Aegeon	PHILLIP GUY-BROMLEY
Duke Solinus	KARL MORGAN DAYMOND
Dromio of Ephesus	CHRISTOPHER TRAKAS
Adriana	KORLISS UECKER
Luciana	SARAH PRING
Eufemio	GARY HARGER
Angelo	JOHN RATH
Lesbia	KATE MCCARNEY
Little Dromio	JURGEN O'BYRNE

National Symphony Orchestra of Ireland
Conductor	MARK SHANAHAN
Director	GILES HAVERGAL
Designer	RUSSELL CRAIG
Lighting	MICHAEL CALF

■ 1992

Der Vampyr *Heinrich Marschner*
24, 27, 30 October, 2, 5, 8 November

Lord Ruthven	WILLIAM PARCHER
Vampire Master	INGO KOLONERICS
Janthe Berkley	PATRICIA MCCAFFREY
Sir John Berkley	PHILLIP GUY-BROMLEY
Berkley's servant	SIMON PREECE
Sir Edgar Aubry	WALTER MACNEIL
Malvina Davenaut	DANIELA BECHLY
Sir Humphrey Davenaut	ALEXANDER MALTA

Emmy Perth	FRANCES LUCEY
George Dibdin	JÜRGEN SACHER
Blunt	JOHANNES VON DUISBURG
Suse	JUTTA WINKLER
Gadshill	JAMES DRUMMOND NELSON
Scrop	NICHOLAS BUXTON
Green	INGO KOLONERICS

Wexford Festival Chorus
Chorus Master	STUART HUTCHINSON
Local Chorus Master	GERARD LAWLOR

National Symphony Orchestra of Ireland
Conductor	GUIDO JOHANNES RUMSTADT
Director	JEAN-CLAUDE AUVRAY
Designer	KENNY MACLELLAN
Lighting Designer	MICHAEL CALF
Choreographer	GAVIN DORRIAN

■ 1993

Cherevichki *Peter Ilyich Tchaikovsky*
14, 17, 20, 23, 26, 29 October

Vakula	ROMAN TSYMBALA
Solokha	VALENTINA CHERBININA
The Devil	LEONID BOLDIN
Chub	VLADIMIR MATORIN
Oksana	MARINA LEVITT
The Mayor	KEITH LATHAM
The Schoolmaster	WJACHESLAW WEINOROWSKI
Panas	RUPERT OLIVER FORBES
His Excellency Potemkin	ANATOLY LOCHAK
Woodsprite	PAUL KEOHONE
Old Cossack	WILLIAM PEEL
Gentleman in waiting	DECLAN KELLY
Master of Ceremonies	ANDREW HAMMOND
Ballerina	ELLA CLARKE

Wexford Festival Chorus
Chorus Master	GREGORY ROSE

National Symphony Orchestra of Ireland
Conductor	ALEXANDER ANISSIMOV
Director	FRANCESCA ZAMBELLO
Designer	BRUNO SCHWENGL
Lighting Designer	DAVID COLMER
Choreographer	GAVIN DORRIAN

■ 1993

Il Barbiere di Siviglia *Giovanni Paisiello*
15, 18, 21, 24, 27, 30 October

Count Almaviva	KJELL MAGNUS SANDVÉ
Figaro	MARK PEDROTTI
Rosina	FRANCES LUCEY
Doctor Bartolo	ENRICO FISSORE
Don Basilio	GABRIELE MONICI
Lo Svegliato	GERARD O'CONNOR
Giovinetto	RUPERT OLIVER FORBES
A notary	KEITH LATHAM
A Judge	JAMES DRUMMOND NELSON
Marcellina	HANNAH FOLEY

National Symphony Orchestra of Ireland
Conductor	CARLA DELFRATE
Director	LUCY BAILEY
Designer	SIMON VINCENZI
Lighting Designer	DAVID COLMER

■ 1993

Zampa *Ferdinand Hérold*
16, 19, 22, 25, 28, 31 October

Camille	MARY MILLS
Alphonse de Monza	BRADLEY WILLIAMS
Ritta	JUTTA WINKLER
Dandolo	ANTOINE NORMAND
Zampa	JOHN DANIECKI
Daniel Capuzzi	VALENTIN JAR
A Corsaire	TOM MCVEIGH
Alice Manfredi	ELLA CLARKE
Lugano	NICKY DUGGAN

Wexford Festival Chorus
Chorus Master	GREGORY ROSE
Local Chorus Master	GERARD LAWLOR

National Symphony Orchestra of Ireland
Conductor	YVES ABEL
Director	TIM HOPKINS
Designer	CHARLES EDWARDS
Lighting Designer	DAVID COLMER

■ 1994

The Demon *Anton Rubinstein*
20, 23, 26, 29 October, 1, 4 November

The Demon	ANATOLY LOCHAK
The Angel	ALISON BROWNER
Tamara	MARINA MESCHERIAKOVA
Prince Gudal	LEONID ZIMNENKO

Prince Sinodal	VALERY SERKIN
Old Servant	RICHARD ROBSON
Nanny	LUDMILLA ANDREW
Messenger	WJACHESLAV WEINOROWSKI

Wexford Festival Chorus
Chorus Master — GREGORY ROSE

National Symphony Orchestra of Ireland
Conductor — ALEXANDER ANISSIMOV

Director — YEFIM MAIZEL
Designer — PAUL STEINBERG
Lighting Designer — DAVID COLMER

■ 1994

La Bohème *Ruggero Leoncavallo*
21, 24, 27, 30 October, 2, 5 November

Musette	MAGALI DAMONTE
Marcello	JEAN-PIERRE FURLAN
Mimi	JUNGWON PARK
Rodolfo	PATRYK WROBLEWSKI
Schaunard	JONATHAN VEIRA
Eufemia	NIAMH MURRAY
Colline	GUIDO LEBRÓN
Gaudenzio	VALENTIN JAR
Barbemuche	GIANCARLO TOSI
Visconte Paolo	FRANK O'BRIEN
Durand	WJACHESLAV WEINOROWSKI
A Lad	IVAN SHARPE
Man from the first floor	SIMON SPENCER WILLIAMS
Clerk	GILES DAVIES
Clerks Wife	EMMA POLLARD
Widow	MARY ROSE LANGFIELD

Wexford Festival Chorus
Chorus Master — GREGORY ROSE

National Symphony Orchestra of Ireland
Coductor — ALBERT ROSEN

Director — RETO NICKLER
Designer — RUSSELL CRAIG
Lighting — DAVID COLMER

■ 1994

Das Liebesverbot *Richard Wagner*
22, 25, 28, 31 October, 3, 6 November

Friedrich	ROBERT HOLZER
Luzio	ROBERT SWENSEN
Claudio	PETER SVENSSON
Antonio	ERIC ASHCRAFT
Angelo	GUIDO LEBRÓN
Isabella	MARIE PLETTE
Mariana	MARIT SAURAMO
Brighella	GIDON SAKS
Danieli	JURIJ KRUGLOV
Dorella	MAJELLA CULLAGH
Pontio Pilato	VALENTIN JAR

Wexford Festival Chorus
Chorus Master — GREGORY ROSE
Local Chorus Master — GERARD LAWLOR

National Symphony Orchestra of Ireland
Conductor — YVES ABEL

Director — DIETER KAEGI
Designer — BRUNO SCHWENGL
Lighting Designer — DAVID COLMER
Choreographer — GAVIN DORRIAN

■ 1995

Saffo *Giovanni Pacini*
19, 22, 25, 28, 31 October, 3 November

Saffo	FRANCESCA PEDACI
Saffo (October 25 & 31)	NICOLETTA ZANINI
Faone	CARLO VENTRE
Alcandro	ROBERTO DE CANDIA
Climene	MARIANA PENTCHEVA
Dirce	GEMMA BERTAGNOLLI
Ippia	ALED HALL
Lisimaco	DAVIDE BARONCHELLI

Wexford Festival Chorus
Chorus Master — LUBOMIR MÁTL

National Symphony Orchestra of Ireland
Conductor — MAURIZIO BENINI

Director, Designer
& Lighting Designer — BENI MONTRESOR

■ 1995

Mayskaya noch' *Nikolay Rimsky-Korsakov*
20, 23, 26, 29 October, 1, 4 November

Golova	VLADIMIR MATORIN
Levko	VSEVELOD GRIVNOV
Hanna	IRINA DOLZHENKO
Golova's Sister-in-Law	FRANCES McCAFFERTY
Kalenik	ANATOLY LOCHAK
The Clerk	MAXIM MIKHAILOV
Distiller	WJACHESLAV WEINOROWSKI
Rusalka	MARINA MESCHERIAKOVA
Rusalki	ANNALISA WINBERG

Rusalki	PAULINE BOURKE
Rusalki	ELENA GUCHINA

Wexford Festival Chorus
Chorus Master — LUBOMIR MÁTL

National Symphony Orchestra of Ireland
Conductor — VLADIMIR JUROWSKI

Director — STEPHEN MEDCALF
Designer — FRANCIS O'CONNOR
Lighting Designer — GUIDO LEVI
Choreographer — KATE FLATT

■ 1995

Iris *Pietro Mascagni*
21, 24, 27, 30 October, 2, 5 November

Iris	MICHIE NAKAMARU
Osaka	LUDOVIT LUDHA
Kyoto	ROY STEVENS
Il Cieco	RICHARD ROBSON
Dhia	CARLA MANEY
Un Merciaiolo & Il Cenciaiuolo	SERGIO PANAJIA
Ballet Dancer	JOY CONSTANTINIDES

Wexford Festival Chorus
Chorus Master — FERGUS SHEIL
Local Chorus Master — GERARD LAWLOR

National Symphony Orchestra of Ireland
Conductor — BRUNO APREA

Director — LORENZO MARIANI
Designer — MAURIZIO BALO
Lighting Designer — GUIDO LEVI
Choreographer — KATE FLATT

■ 1996

Parisina *Gaetano Donizetti*
17, 20, 23, 26, 29 October, 1 November

Parisina	ALEXANDRINA PENDATCHANSKA
Parisina (October 20)	MONICA COLONNA
Ugo	AMADEO MORETTI
Azzo	ROBERTO SERVILLE
Ernesto	RICHARD ROBSON
Imelda	DANIELA BARCELLONA

Wexford Festival Chorus
Chorus Master — LUBOMIR MÁTL

National Symphony Orchestra of Ireland
Conductor — MAURIZIO BENINI
Conductor (Oct 29 & Nov 01) — ROBERTO POLASTRI

Director — STEFANO VIZIOLI
Designer & Lighting Designer — ULDERICO MANANI

■ 1996

L'Étoile du Nord *Giacomo Meyerbeer*
18, 21, 24, 27, 30 October, 2 November

Catherina	ELIZABETH FUTRAL
Peter the Great	VLADIMIR OGNEV
Prascovia	DARINA TAKOVA
Danilowitz	ALED HALL
Gritzenko	CHRISTOPHER MALTMAN
George	JUAN DIEGO FLOREZ
Natalia	AGNETE MUNK RASMUSSEN
Ekimona	PATRIZIA CIGNA
Ismailoff	ROBERT LEE
Reynold	FERNAND BERNADI
Yermoloff	LUIS LEDESMA

Wexford Festival Chorus
Chorus Master — LUBOMIR MÁTL

National Symphony Orchestra of Ireland
Conductor — VLADIMIR JUROWSKI

Director, Designer & Lighting Designer — DENIS KRIEF
Choreographer — GIOVANNI DE CICCO

■ 1996

Šárka *Zdenek Fibich*
19, 22, 25, 28, 31 October, 3 November

Šárka	SVETELINA VASSILEVA
Ctirad	LUDOVIT LUDHA
Vlasta	DENISA ŠLEPKOVSKÁ
Prince Premysl	ANATOLY LOCHAK
Vitoraz	RICHARD ROBSON
Lybina	GIUSEPPINA PIUNTI
Mlada	JULIET BOOTH
Svatava	GISELLE ALLEN
Radka	MARGARETA HILLERUD
Hosta	KIM-MARIE WOODHOUSE
Castava	CINZIA DE MOLA

Wexford Festival Chorus
Chorus Master — LUBOMIR MÁTL

National Symphony Orchestra of Ireland
Conductor — DAVID AGLER

Director — INGA LEVANT
Designer & Lighting Designer — CHARLES EDWARDS
Costume Designer — BRIGITTE REIFFENSTUEL

1997

Elena Da Feltre *Saverio Mercadante*
16, 19, 22, 25, 28, 31 October

Elena	MONICA COLONNA
Guido	NICOLA ULIVIERI
Ubaldo	CESARE CATANI
Sigifredo	STEFANO RINALDI-MILIANI
Imberga	ELENA ROSSI
Boemondo	LUIGI PETRONI
Gualtiero	LONRENZO MUZZI

Wexford Festival Chorus
Chorus Master — LUBOMIR MÁTL

National Symphony Orchestra of Ireland
Conductor — MAURIZIO BENINI

Director — SONJA FRISELL
Designer — MAROUAN DIB
Lighting Designer — VINCENZO RAPONI

1997

Rusalka *Alexander Dargomizhsky*
17, 20, 23, 26, 29 October, 1 November

Natasha /Rusalka	ANNA MARIA CHIURI
Melnik the Miller	MAXIM MIKHAILOV
Knagi /The Prince	ALESSANDRO SAFINA
Knagina /The Princess	ANNIE VAVRILLE
Svat	MASSIMILIANO GAGLIARDO
Olga	LJUBA CHUCHROVA
Rusalotchka/Loreley	KATIA TREBELEVA
A Huntsman	STEVEN BOYDALL
A Villageman	DECLAN KELLY

Wexford Festival Chorus
Chorus Master — LUBOMIR MÁTL

National Symphony Orchestra of Ireland
Conductor — PAUL MÄGI
Conductor (Oct 26 & 29) — ALEXANDRE VOLOSCHUK

Director — DEMITRI BERTMAN
Set Designer — IGOR NEZNY
Costume Designer — TATYANA TULUBIEVA
Lighting Designer — VINCENZO RAPONI
Choreographer — ALESSANDRA PANZAVOLTA

1997

La Fiamma *Ottorino Respighi*
18, 21, 24, 27, 30 October, 2 November

Silvana	ELMIRA MAGOMEDOVA
Donello	JURI ALEXEEV
Basilio	ANATOLY LOCHAK
Eudossia	DANIELA BARCELLONA
Monica	GIUSEPPINA PIUNTI
Agnese di Cervia	PAOLO PELLICIARI
Il Vescovo / L'Esorcista	CARLO LEPORE
Agata	TEREZA MATLOVA
Lucilla	ELENA BELFIORE
Sabina	JOANNA CAMPION
Zoe	DOREEN CURRAN
Una madre	DAGMAR BUNDZOVA
Un cherico	DECLAN KELLY

Wexford Festival Chorus
Chorus Master — LUBOMIR MÁTL

Wexford Festival Childrens' Choir
Choir Master — GERARD LAWLOR

National Symphony Orchestra of Ireland
Conductor — ENRIQUE MAZZOLA

Director — FRANCO RIPA DI MEANA
Set Designer — EDOARDO SANCHI
Choreographer — ALESSANDRA PANZAVOLTA
Costume Designer — STEVE ALMERIGHI
Lighting Designer — VINCENZO RAPONI

1998

Fosca *Carlos Gomes*
15, 18, 21, 24, 27, 30 October

Fosca	ELMIRA VEDA
Cambro	ANATOLY LOCHAK
Delia	GIUSEPPINA PIUNTI
Paolo	FERNANDO DEL VALLE
Gajolo	TIGRAN MARTIROSSIAN
Giotta	ALESSANDRO GUERZONI
Doge	COLIN IVESON

Wexford Festival Chorus
Chorus Master — LUBOMIR MÁTL

National Symphony Orchestra of Ireland
Conductor — ALEXANDER ANISSIMOV

Director, Set & Costume Designer — GIOVANNI AGOSTINUCCI
Assistant Set & Costume Designer — GIOVANNA MONTGOMERY
Lighting Designer — VINCENZO RAPONI

1998

Šarlatán *Pavel Haas*
16, 19, 22, 25, 28, 31 October

Pustrpalk	Luca Grassi
Rosina	Louise Walsh
Bachelor	Ludovit Ludha
Sourmilk	Peter Wedd
Cobweb	Alessandro Guerzoni
First Student	Julian Jensen
Town Physician	Simon Wilding
Fire Eater	Alberto Janelli
Snake Charmer	František Zahradníček
Second Student	Jiři Vinklárek
Third Student	Julian Tovey
Amaranta	Viktoria Vizin
Jochimus	Leigh Melrose
Jochimus Servant	Alberto Janelli
Monster/Inn Keeper	Jeong Won Lee
King	David Marsh
Another man	Radek Prügl

Wexford Festival Chorus
Chorus Master — Lubomir Mátl

National Symphony Orchestra of Ireland
Conductor — Israel Yinon

Director — John Abulafia
Assistant Director — Orpha Phelan
Designer — Fotini Dimou
Lighting Designer — Vincenzo Raponi

1998

I Cavalieri di Ekebù *Riccardo Zandonai*
17, 20, 23, 26, 29 October, 1 November

Giosta Berling	Dario Volonté
La Comandante	Francesca Franci
Anna	Alida Barbasini
Sintram	Maxim Mikhailov
Cristiano	Victor Chernomortzev
Samzelius	David Marsh
Liecrona	Joseph Calleja
Un'ostessa	Tea Demurishvili
Una fanciulla	Irina Lasareva
Ruster	Julian Jensen
Julius	Peter Wedd
Fuchs	Julian Tovey
Rutger	Colin Iveson
Everardo	František Zahradníček
Wemburgo	Simon Wilding
Kenvellere	Alberto Janelli
Kristoffer	Jiři Vinklárek
Berencreuz	Jeong Won Lee

Wexford Festival Chorus
Chorus Master — Lubomir Mátl

National Symphony Orchestra of Ireland
Conductor — Daniele Callegari

Director — Gabriele Vacis
Set Designer — Francesco Calcagnini
Costume Designer — Hilary Lewis
Lighting Designer — Vincenzo Raponi

1999

Die Königin von Saba *Karl Goldmark*
14, 17, 20, 23, 26, 29 October

Königin von Saba	Cornelia Helfricht
Assad	Mauro Nicoletti
Assad	Valerij Popov
Konig Salomon	Max Wittges
Hohepriester	Piotr Nowacki
Sulamith	Inka Rinn
Astaroth	Tereza Mátlová
Baal-Hanaan	Vladimir Glushchak

Wexford Festival Chorus
Chorus Master — Lubomir Mátl

National Symphony Orchestra of Ireland
Conductor — Claude Schnitzler

Director — Patrick Mailler
Designer — Massimo Gasparon
Lighting Designer — Vincenzo Raponi

1999

Straszny Dwór *Stanislaw Moniuszko*
15, 18, 21, 24, 27, 30 October

Miecznik	Zenon Kowalski
Hanna	Iwona Hossa
Jadwiga	Viktoria Vizin
Stefan	Dariusz Stachura
Zbigniew	Jacek Janiszewski
Cześnikowa	Elizabeth Woods
Maciej	Zbigniew Macias
Skołuba	Piotr Nowacki
Pan Damazy	Leszek Świdzinski
Marta	Roberta Zelnickova
Grześ	Petr Frýbert
Stara Niewiasta	Roberta Zelnickova

Wexford Festival Chorus
Chorus Master — Lubomir Mátl

National Symphony Orchestra of Ireland
Conductor — David Jones

Director — Michal Znaniecki

Set Designer	Francesco Calcagnini
Costume Consultant	Dalia Gallico
Lighting Designer	Vincenzo Raponi
Choreographer	Isadora Weiss

■ 1999

Siberia *Umberto Giordano*
16, 19, 22, 25, 28, 31 October

Stephana	Elena Zelenskaia
Vassili	Dario Volonté
Gleby	Walter Donati
Nikona	Claudia Marchi
Il Principe Alexis/Il Cosacco	Massimo Giordano
Walinoff/Il Governatore	Eldar Aliev
La Fanciulla	Chloë Wright
Ivan/Il Sergente	Darren Abrahams
Il Capitano/L'Ispettore	František Zahradníček
Miskinsky/L'Invalido	Zbigniew Macias

Wexford Festival Chorus
Chorus Master — Lubomir Mátl

National Symphony Orchestra of Ireland
Conductor — Daniele Callegari

Director	Fabio Sparvoli
Set Designer	Giorgio Ricchelli
Costume Designer	Alessandra Torella
Lighting Designer	Vincenzo Raponi
Choreographer	Isadora Weiss

■ 2000

Orleanskaya deva *Pytor Il'yich Tchaikovsky*
19, 22, 25, 28 October, 3 November

Jeanne d'Arc	Lada Biriucov
King Charles VII	Juri Alexeev
Lionel	Igor Tarassov
Thibaut d'Arc	Aleksander Teliga
Agnès Sorel	Ermonela Jaho
Raymond	Ayhan Ardà
Dunois	Igor Morozov
Archbishop	Andrei Antonov
Bertrand	Sergio Foresti
A Warrior/Lauret	František Zahradníček
An Angel's voice	Katia Trebeleva

Wexford Festival Chorus
Chorus Master — Lubomir Mátl

National Symphony Orchestra of Ireland
Conductor — Daniele Callegari

Director — Massimo Gasparon

Designer	Massimo Gasparon
Lighting Designer	Rupert Murray

■ 2000

Si j'étais roi *Adolphe Adam*
20, 23, 26, 29 October, 1, 4 November

Zéphoris	Joseph Calleja
Néméa	Iwona Hossa
Le Roi	Roberto Accurso
Piféar	Darren Abrahams
Zélide	Tereza Mátlová
Kadoor	Igor Morozov
Zizel	Nicola Alaimo
Une Choryphée	Fiona O'Reilly
Atar	Ales Mihalik
Dancer	Dara Pierce
Dancer	Emma Martin

Wexford Festival Chorus
Chorus Master — Lubomir Mátl

National Symphony Orchestra of Ireland
Conductor — David Agler

Director & Choreographer	Renaud Doucet
Set Designer	André Barbe
Costume Designer	Huguette Barbet-Blanchard
Lighting Designer	Rupert Murray

■ 2000

Conchita *Riccardo Zandonai*
21, 24, 27, 30 October, 2, 5 November

Conchita	Monica di Siena
Mateo	Renzo Zulian
La Madre	Agnieszka Zwierko
Estella	Katia Trebeleva
Dolores	Alison Buchanan
Rufina	Joanna Campion
La Sorvegliante	Fiona Murphy
L'Ispettore	Aleksander Teliga
Garcia	Nicola Alaimo

Wexford Festival Chorus
Chorus Master — Lubomir Mátl

National Symphony Orchestra of Ireland
Conductor — Marcello Rota

Director	Corrado D'Elia
Set Designer	Fabrizio Palla
Costume Designer	Steve Almerighi
Lighting Designer	Rupert Murray

■ *2001*

Alessandro Stradella *Friedrich Flotow*
18, 21, 24, 27, 30 October, 2 November

Alessandro Stradella	STEFANO COSTA
Bassi	ANDREI ANTONOV
Leonore	EKATERINA MOROZOVA
Malvolio	FRANTIŠEK ZAHRADNÍČEK
Barbarino	DECLAN KELLY

Wexford Festival Chorus
Chorus Master   LUBOMIR MÁTL

National Philharmonic Orchestra of Belarus

Conductor	DANIELE CALLEGARI
Director	THOMAS DE MALLET BURGESS
Designer	JULIAN MCGOWAN
Lighting Designer	GIUSEPPE DI IORIO
Choreographer	LYNNE HOCKNEY

■ *2001*

Jakobín *Antonin Dvořák*
19, 22, 25, 28, 31 October, 3 November

Count Vilém of Harasov	VALENTIN PIVOVAROV
Bohus	MARKUS WERBA
Adolf	ALESSANDRO GRATO
Julie	TATIANA MONOGAROVA
Filip	MIRCO PALAZZI
Jiri	MICHAL LEHOTSKY
Benda	ALASDAIR ELLIOT
Terinka	MARIANA PANOVA
Lotinka	REBECCA SHARP

Wexford Festival Chorus
Chorus Master   LUBOMIR MÁTL

The Young Wexford Singers
Childrens' Chorus Master   EANNA MCKENNA

National Philharmonic Orchestra of Belarus

Conductor	ALEXANDRE VOLOSCHUK
Director	MICHAEL MCCAFFREY
Designer	PAUL EDWARDS
Lighting Designer	GIUSEPPE DI IORIO
Choreographer	LYNNE HOCKNEY

■ *2001*

Sapho *Jules Massenet*
20, 23, 26, 29 October, 1, 4 November

Fanny Legrand	GIUSEPPINA PIUNTI
Jean Gaussin	BRANDON JOVANOVICH
Divonne	AGATA BIENKOWSKA
Césaire	MASSIMILIANO GAGLIARDO
Irène	ERMONELA JAHO
Caoudal	LUCA SALSI
La Borderie	ANGEL PAZOS
Le patron du restaurant	NICOLAS COURJAL

Wexford Festival Chorus
Chorus Master   LUBOMIR MÁTL

National Philharmonic Orchestra of Belarus

Conductor	JEAN-LUC TINGAUD
Director	FABIO SPARVOLI
Set Designer	GIORGIO RICCHELLI
Costume Designer	ALESSANDRA TORELLA
Lighting Designer	GIUSEPPE DI IORIO

Index of Artists 1951 – 2001

Abel, Yves 1993, 1994
Abrahams, Darren 1999, 2000
Abulafia, John 1998
Accurso, Roberto 2000
Adams, Christopher 1983
Adams, Jennifer 1983
Adani, Mariella 1959
Agai, Karola 1964
Agler, David 1996, 2000
Agostinucci, Giovanni 1998
Aguade, Angela 1977
Alaimo, Nicola 2000
Alberti, Walter 1964
Alexeev, Juri 1997, 2000
Aliberti, Lucia 1979, 1981, 1983
Aliev, Eldar 1999
Allen, Giselle 1996
Allen, Paschal 1966
Almerighi, Steve 1997, 2000
Alvares, Eduardo 1983, 1984
Andrew, Ludmilla 1990, 1994
Andrew, Milla 1970
Angioletti, Mariella 1958, 1959, 1961
Anissimov, Alexander 1993, 1994, 1998
Anthony, Trevor 1959
Antonov, Andrei 2000, 2001
Aprea, Bruno 1995
Aragall, Giacomo 1964
Archer, Robin 1968
Ardà, Ayhan 2000
Arden-Griffith, Paul 1980, 1989
Armiliato, Fabio 1987
Armstrong, James 1965
Arnould, Bernard 1975
Arthur, Maurice 1968, 1976
Ashcraft, Eric 1994
Ashe, Rosemary 1983
Atherton, David 1970
Audsley, Sarah 1988
Auvray, Jean-Claude 1975, 1990, 1992
Ayldon, John 1984

Aylwin, Richard 1990

Baar, Ian 1989
Babl, Wolfgang 1991
Bailey, Jean 1985
Bailey, Lucy 1989, 1993
Bailey, Norman 1988
Baillie, Peter 1968
Bainbridge, Elizabeth 1959, 1990
Baker, Alice 1988
Baker, Janet 1959
Bakker, Marco 1971, 1972
Bakst, Lawrence 1985
Baleani, Silvia 1973
Balkwill, Bryan 1953, 1954, 1955, 1956, 1957, 1958, 1961
Balo, Maurizio 1995
Bamert, Matthias 1979
Banbury, Frith 1966
Bandi, Janos 1988
Bankes-Jones, William 1989
Bannatyne-Scott, Brian 1989
Baran, Ayhan 1966
Barasorda, Antonio 1975
Barbasini, Alida 1998
Barbe, André 2000
Barbet-Blanchard, Huguette 2000
Barbier, Guy 1971, 1973
Barcellona, Daniela 1996, 1997
Barnard, Richard 1971
Baronchelli, Davide 1995
Barrell, David 1987
Barrett, Richard 1975
Bartha, Alfonz 1963
Bartleet, David 1986
Bartz, Axel 1978
Bateman, Frederick 1967
Bates, Terry John 1983, 1984, 1985, 1986, 1987, 1988, 1989, 1990
Bax, Erica 1964
Beauchamp, Michael 1972, 1986
Beavan, David 1979
Bechly, Daniela 1986, 1992

Belfiore, Elena 1997
Bell, Robin 1965
Bellini, Gabriele 1983
Benedict, Anna 1975, 1977
Benelli, Ugo 1965, 1966, 1969, 1970, 1978, 1981, 1983
Benini, Maurizio 1995, 1996, 1997
Bernadi, Fernand 1996
Bertagnolli, Gemma 1995
Bertman, Demitri 1997
Besch, Anthony 1955, 1961, 1967, 1971, 1972
Bickerstaff, Robert 1970
Bienkowska, Agata 2001
Biriucov, Lada 2000
Bjornsen, Maria 1972, 1973
Blacker, Thetis 1954
Blades, Christopher 1982
Blane, Sue 1972, 1973, 1978, 1979
Blanzat, Anne-Marie 1971
Boer, Nico 1980
Boerlage, Frans 1958, 1959
Bohan, Edmund 1964
Boldin, Leonid 1993
Bolton, Andrea 1988
Bond, Jane 1970, 1971
Bonifaccio, Maddalena 1965
Booth, Juliet 1996
Booth, Thomas 1992
Borthayre, Jean 1961
Bottazzo, Pietro 1964, 1967, 1968
Bottone, Bonaventura 1977, 1978, 1979
Bourke, Pauline 1995
Bowden, Pamela 1967
Bowen, Maurice 1965
Boyaciyan, Kevork 1974
Boydall, Steven 1997
Boyer, Antonio 1966
Bradford, William 1973
Brandt, Dennis 1964, 1967
Branisteanu, Horiana 1973
Brazzi, Jean 1967
Bremner, Anthony 1970, 1971
Brennan, Yvonne 1989, 1990, 1991
Brewer, Bruce 1988

Bride Street Wexford Boys Choir 1980, 1981
Brogan, Deirdre 1979
Broome, Oliver 1965, 1987
Browne, James 1951
Browne, Oliver 1966
Browne, Sandra 1975
Browner, Alison 1988, 1991, 1994
Brunner, Evelyn 1982
Bruscantini, Sesto 1977, 1979, 1981
Bryan, Robert 1971, 1972
Brydon, Roderick 1974, 1975
Buchanan, Alison 2000
Bundzova, Dagmar 1997
Buoso, Ennio 1979
Burrowes, Norma 1971
Burt, Robert 1989
Burton, Amy 1989
Bury, John 1975
Busher, Jimmy 1979
Busterud, James 1989
Butlin, Roger 1971, 1977, 1978, 1979
Buxton, David 1990
Buxton, Nicholas 1992
Bybee, Luretta 1989
Byran, Robert 1972
Byrne, Connall 1961

Caddy, Ian 1975
Caforio, Armando 1982
Calabrese, Franco 1954
Calcagnini, Francesco 1998, 1999
Calf, Michael 1991, 1992
Calkins, Mark 1990
Callegari, Daniele 1998, 1999, 2000, 2001
Calleja, Joseph 1998, 2000
Campion, Joanna 1997, 2000
Cangalovic, Miroslav 1965
Cant, Anne 1971, 1976
Cantelo, April 1956, 1957
Caproni, Bruno 1987
Card, June 1971
Cardon, Stéphan 1987

150

Carl, Joseph 1952, 1953, 1954, 1956, 1957
Carlin, Mario 1968
Carsen, Robert 1987
Cash, Jessica 1975
Cashmore, John 1984
Casula, Maria 1967, 1968
Catani, Cesare 1997
Cavanagh, Brendan 1980, 1981, 1982, 1983, 1984, 1985, 1987, 1990
Ceccato, Aldo 1968
Cemore, Alan 1988
Cervena, Sona 1972, 1973
Cervenka, John 1980
Chapman, Roger 1980
Chateau, Christiane 1975
Cherbinina, Valentina 1993
Chernomortzev, Victor 1998
Chitty, Alison 1991
Chiuri, Anna Maria 1997
Christiansen, James 1966
Chuchrova, Ljuba 1997
Cicco, Giovanni de 1996
Ciesinski, Kristine 1988
Cigna, Patrizia 1996
Cimino, John 1990
Ciurdea, Teodor 1986
Clabassi, Plinio 1958
Clare, Gavin 1988
Clarey, Cynthia 1985, 1986, 1987
Clarke, Ella 1993
Clarke, Mary 1989
Cleobury, Nicholas 1981
Cleveland, Kenneth 1970, 1971, 1974, 1975, 1977
Clifton, Geoffrey 1955, 1956, 1958
Cloward, Constance 1983
Coffey, Fergal 1979
Cognet, Andre 1990, 1991
Colavecchia, Franco 1975
Cold, Ulrik 1981
Colfer, Eoin 1979
Collins, Anne 1976
Colmer, David 1993, 1994
Colonna, Monica 1996, 1997
Comboy, Ian 1976
Connell, Elizabeth 1972
Cononovici, Magdalena 1979, 1980
Constantinides, Joy 1995

Cook, Kandis 1980
Cooper, Lawrence 1980
Copley, John 1968, 1969
Cornwell, Joseph 1986
Cossotto, Fiorenza 1958
Costa, Stefano 2001
Cotlow, Marilyn 1954
Courjal, Nicolas 2001
Cowdrick, Kathryn 1991
Cox, John 1967, 1968, 1969, 1970, 1971
Craig, Douglas 1963
Craig, Russell 1981, 1987, 1992, 1994
Creasy, Philip 1981
Creffield, Rosanne 1982
Crist, Richard 1991
Crochot, Michel 1964
Crook, Stephen 1990
Crowther, Melanie 1969, 1970, 1971, 1972, 1973, 1974
Csonka, Zsuzsanna 1991
Cucchio, Marina 1958
Cullagh, Majella 1994
Culshaw, Bernard 1969, 1984
Cumberland, David 1990
Curran, Doreen 1997
Curtis, Alan 1985
Cuthbert, James G 1951
Cutts, Alan 1976, 1977, 1978, 1979

Dales, Ellen 1958
Dallamangas, Cristiano 1952, 1953, 1956
Daltin, Renata 1987
Dalton, Elisabeth 1970, 1971
Daly, Tony 1964
Damonte, Magali 1994
Daniecki, John 1989, 1993
Davenport, Glyn 1977
Davià, Federico 1964, 1965, 1970
Davidson, Geoffrey 1988, 1989
Davies, Derick 1962, 1963
Davies, Giles 1994
Davies, Joan 1974, 1975, 1987, 1988
Davies, Maldwyn 1982
Davison, Peter J 1989

Day, Richard 1955
De Almeida, Antonio 1963, 1964
De Candia, Roberto 1995
de Javelin, Sara 1971
de Leon, Jorge 1990
de Mallet Burgess, Thomas 2001
de Mola, Cinzia 1996
de Monti, Matteo 1975
de Narké, Victor 1967
de Peyer, Adrian 1962, 1963
de Simone, Bruno 1988
De Tarczynska, Halinka 1954
Del Monte, Carlo 1958
del Valle, Fernando 1998
Delacôte, Jacques 1974
Delfrate, Carla 1993
d'Elia, Corrado 2000
Dell'Acqua, Iris 1980
Dell'Acqua, Irish 1975
Delrez, Gerard 1978
DeMain, John 1980
Dempsey, Martin 1963
Dempsey, Shirley 1990
Demurishvili, Tea 1998
Desideri, Carlo 1981
di Iorio, Giuseppe 2001
di Siena, Monica 2000
Dib, Marouan 1997
Dickerson, Bernard 1973
Dickie, Murray 1951
Diego Florez, Juan 1996
Dimou, Fotini 1998
Dixon, Helen 1978
Dobbs, Mattiwilda 1965
Dobson, John 1959
Doghan, Philip 1986
Doghan, Philip 1987, 1988
Dolzhenko, Irina 1995
Donati, Walter 1999
Donlan, Brian 1968, 1970, 1971, 1986
Donnellan, Declan 1985
Donnelly, Malcolm 1977, 1978
Donnelly, Patrick 1987
Dorrian, Gavin 1991, 1992, 1993, 1994
Doucet, Renaud 2000
Douglas, Nigel 1966
Drabowicz, Wojciech 1990
Drennan, Noel 1972

Drummond Nelson, James 1992, 1993
du Plessis, Christian 1972, 1984
Dublin City Ballet 1987
Dugdale, Sandra 1976, 1991
Duggan, Nicky 1993
Dunne, Veronica 1962
Dunphy, Ross 1988
Dupleix, Denise 1968
Dupouy, Jean 1977
Dvorkin, Arnold 1976

Ebert, Carl 1965
Ebert, Judith 1965
Ebert, Peter 1952, 1953, 1954, 1956, 1957, 1961, 1962, 1963, 1964, 1965
Eda-Pierre, Christiane 1970, 1971, 1972
Edwards, Charles 1992, 1993, 1996
Edwards, Paul 2001
Egerton, Francis 1965, 1966, 1974, 1990
Egerton, Francis 1966, 1974, 1990
Elder, Anton 1973
Elkins, Margreta 1974
Elliot, Alasdair 2001
Ellis, Brent 1972
Elvin, William 1970
Engels, Johan 1984
Enigarescu, Octav 1965
Ensemble fom Radio Telefís Éireann Symphony 1970
Ercolani, Renato 1966
Esparza, Elfego 1968, 1970
Esswood, Paul 1975
Evans, Geraint 1957
Evans, John 1961
Evans, Joseph 1988, 1989
Eve, Michael 1958

Fairs, Alan 1988
Farrell, Gordon 1966
Fay, Colin 1973
Feeney, Angela 1981
Feighan, Therese 1987, 1989
Fielding, David 1974, 1976, 1983, 1988
Fieldsend, David 1972
Finn, Marian 1981
Fischer, Gyorgy 1984

Fisher, Adrian 1989
Fissore, Enrico 1966, 1993
Flanagan, John 1972
Flatt, Kate 1995
Foley, Hannah 1993
Forbes, Garrick 1989
Forbes, Rupert Oliver 1993
Forbes-Lane, Andrew 1989
Ford, Bruce 1986
Forest, Michael 1988
Forest, Peter 1973
Forcsti, Sergio 2000
Franci, Francesca 1998
Fraser, John 1969, 1970, 1974
Fredman, Myer 1962, 1963, 1966, 1969, 1971
Freni, Mirella 1962
Friel, Tony 1984
Frisell, Sonja 1997
Fryatt, John 1972
Frýbert, Petr 1999
Fuller, Yvonne 1970
Furlan, Jean-Pierre 1994
Futral, Elizabeth 1996

Gagliardo, Massimiliano 1997, 2001
Gale, Elizabeth 1978
Gallacher, Andrew 1982, 1983
Gallea, Christina 1968
Gallico, Dalia 1999
Gallois, Henri 1977, 1978
Garcia, Jose 1992
Garcisanz, Isabel 1968
Gardner, Jake 1987
Garrett, Eric 1975
Garrett, Lesley 1980, 1981
Gasparon, Massimo 1999, 2000
Gastambide, Ariane 1982
Gauci, Miriam 1987
Gaynor, James 1965
Geliot, Michael 1970, 1971, 1972
Gelling, Philip 1982
George, Donald 1989
Gibbs, John 1985
Gierster, Hans 1955
Gilbert, Terry 1978
Gimenez, Raul 1984, 1985
Giordano, Massimo 1999
Giron May, Luis 1987

Gismondo, Giuseppe 1963
Gloster, Dermod 1965
Glover, Jane 1975, 1977
Glushchak, Vladimir 1999
Golding, Richard 1964, 1965
Golvala, Minoo 1965
Gomez, Jill 1969, 1970, 1974, 1983
Gonzalez, Manuel 1973
Gordoni, Viriginia 1966
Gossage, Julie 1991
Grant, Pauline 1968
Grassi, Luca 1998
Grato, Alessandro 2001
Greevy, Bernadette 1962, 1969, 1977, 1980, 1982, 1985
Griffiths, Gwyn 1954, 1955, 1956, 1957
Grimsley, Greer 1989
Grisales, Ernesto 1991
Grivnov, Vsevelod 1995
Guchina, Elena 1995
Guerzoni, Alessandro 1998
Gui, Henri 1967, 1968
Guidarini, Marco 1988, 1989
Guiot, Andrea 1961
Gullino, Walter 1967
Guschlbauer, Theodor 1968
Guy-Bromley, Phillip 1988, 1992

Hadji Mischev, Anna 1963
Hadji Mischev, Michael 1962, 1963, 1970, 1973
Hall, Aled 1995, 1996
Hamilton, Charles 1983
Hamm, Theresa 1990
Hammond, Andrew 1992, 1993
Hancock, Leonard 1976
Hanley, Regina 1990
Hanlon, Michel 1951
Hannan, Eilene 1977
Hargan, Alison 1980
Harger, Gary 1992
Harling, Stuart 1975
Harper, Heather 1955
Harrhy, Eiddwen 1974
Harrhy, Paul 1989
Harris, Dinah 1978
Harrison, Maxwell 1978

Hartle, Enid 1969, 1970
Haskin, Howard 1982, 1983
Hastings, Emily 1978
Havergal, Giles 1992
Hayes, Dermot 1981
Hayes, Jamie 1990, 1991
Haythornthwaite, Edward 1991
Haythornthwaite, Samuel 1991
Heap, Douglas 1979, 1980
Helfricht, Cornelia 1999
Hemsley, Thomas 1955
Hendriks, Marijke 1986
Hermiston, Nancy 1984
Hetherington, Elizabeth 1990
Hickox, Richard 1991
Hidjov, Plamen 1988
Hillerud, Margareta 1996
Hinds, Andy 1984
Hoch, Beverly 1986
Hockney, Lynne 2001
Hoekman, Guus 1963
Hoffman, Paula 1989
Holmes, John 1956
Holzer, Robert 1994
Hooker, Elaine 1968
Hope, Julian 1977, 1978, 1979, 1983
Hopkins, Tim 1993
Horaček, Jaroslav 1967
Hore, Mrs C 1951, 1952, 1953, 1954, 1955, 1955, 1956, 1957, 1958, 1959, 1961, 1962, 1963, 1964, 1965, 1966
Hose, Anthony 1967
Hossa, Iwona 1999, 2000
Howell, Roger 1984
Howells, Anne 1973
Howells, Susan 1971
Howitt, Barbara 1956, 1957
Hudson, Richard 1986
Hughes, Janet 1970, 1972
Hughes, Mick 1982, 1983, 1984, 1985
Humilis O.F.M., Rev Fr 1962
Hunt, Alexandra 1972
Hunt, Annabel 1973
Hunt, Marilyn 1983
Hutchinson, Stuart 1992
Hux, Christopher 1991

Hytner, Nicholas 1982

Illing, Rosamund 1982
Irish National Ballet 1985
Isley, Christine 1980
Iveson, Colin 1998

Jaho, Ermonela 2000, 2001
Jaia, Gianna 1958
Jampolis, Neil Peter 1988
Janelli, Alberto 1998
Janiszewski, Jacek 1999
Jansen, Neil 1983
Janski, Stefan 1984, 1985
Jar, Valentin 1985, 1986, 1993, 1994
Jarvis, Tessa 1973
Jenkins, Angela 1963
Jenkins, Neil 1989
Jenkins, Newell 1982
Jennings, Gloria 1965
Jensen, Julian 1998
Joel, Emmanuel 1990
Johnson, Patricia 1984
Johnston, David 1964, 1965
Joly, Simon 1981, 1982, 1983, 1985, 1988, 1990
Jones, David 1999
Jones, Keith 1976
Jones, Richard 1986
Joseph, Justin 1992
Jotti, Renza 1967
Jovanovich, Brandon 2001
Judd, James 1976, 1977, 1978, 1979, 1980, 1981
Judd, Wilfred 1980
Jurowski, Vladimir 1995, 1996

Kaegi, Dieter 1994
Kelley, Frank 1991
Kelly, Declan 1993, 1997, 2001
Kelly, Paul Austin 1991
Kelston, Lucia 1969
Kember, Gordon 1968, 1973
Kemmer, Mariette 1990
Kemp, Brian 1982, 1983
Kennedy, Roderick 1979, 1980
Kenny, Courtney 1963, 1964, 1978, 1984
Kentish, John 1955
Keohone, Paul 1993

Kern, Patricia 1956, 1957, 1958
Kerr, Virginia 1981, 1984
Keyes, Statia 1951
Krief, Denis 1996
Kingsley, Margaret 1976
Kitchiner, John 1970
Klasicki, Victoria 1976
Knight, Gillian 1975, 1990
Kolonerics, Ingo 1992
Kong, Fan-Chang 1992
Kopp, Miroslav 1988
Korosec, Ladko 1965
Kowalski, Zenon 1999
Kruglov, Jurij 1994
Krutikov, Mikhail 1987
Kuhlmann, Kathleen 1986
Kyzlink, Jan 1972

Lafon, Brigitte 1990
Lancaster, Osbert 1959, 1961
Landry, Rosemarie 1982
Lane, Aideen 1978
Lane, Gloria 1963
Langdon, Michael 1976
Langfield, Mary Rose 1994
Langridge, Philip 1965, 1975
Langton, Sunny Joy 1985
Large, Graham 1976, 1979, 1980, 1981
Lasareva, Irina 1998
Latham, Keith 1992, 1993
Latham-Koenig, Jan 1987
Laughlin, Roy 1987, 1988
Lavani, Carmen 1977
Law, Jane 1980
Lawlor, Gerard 1980, 1981, 1982, 1983, 1984, 1985, 1986, 1987, 1988, 1989, 1990, 1991, 1992, 1993, 1994, 1995, 1997
Lawlor, Thomas 1971, 1989, 1990
Le Maigat, Pierre-Yves 1987
Lebrón, Guido 1994
Lecca, Marie-Jeanne 1985
Ledbetter, Victor 1991
Ledesma, luis 1996
Lee, Lynda 1991
Lee, Robert 1996
Lee, Soo-Bee 1964
Lees, Susan 1972, 1983

Leeson-Williams, Nigel 1990, 1991
Leggate, Robin 1974
Lehotsky, Michal 2001
Leiferkus, Sergei 1982, 1983, 1984, 1986
Lepore, Carlo 1997
Levant, Inga 1996
Levi, Guido 1995
Levitt, Marina 1993
Lewis, Griffith 1959
Lewis, Hilary 1998
Lewis, Michael 1977
Lewis, William 1986
Libby, Patrick 1973, 1976
Lightfoot, Peter 1988
Ligi, Josella 1985
Lindermeier, Elizabeth 1955
Link, Kurt 1992
Linstedt, Elaine 1978
Livingstone, Claire 1979
Livingstone, Laureen 1970
Lloyd, Powell 1951
Lloyd-Davies, John 1991
Lloyd-Jones, David 1967, 1968, 1969, 1970
Lloyd-Morgan, Richard 1983, 1984
Lo Forese, Angelo 1969
Loch Garman Silver Band 1990
Lochak, Anatoly 1993, 1994, 1995, 1996, 1997, 1998
Lochtie, Bruce 1966
Lockwood, Victor 1978
Loehle, Peter 1989
Lowney, Joe 1965
Lucey, Frances 1992, 1993
Luchetti, Veriano 1965
Ludha, Ludovit 1995, 1996, 1998

MacArthur, Helen 1974
MacDonald, William 1972
Macias, Zbigniew 1999
MacKay, Morag 1985
Mackerras, Charles 1958, 1959
Mackey, Hugh 1991
Mackie, Neil 1981
MacLellan, Kenny 1990, 1992
Mac Liammóir, Micheál 1959

MacNally, John 1964
MacNeil, Walter 1992
Madden, Tony 1981
Mägi, Paul 1997
Magiera, Leone 1972
Magomedova, Elmira 1997
Magri, Alexander 1974, 1976
Maguire, James 1976
Maher, Ruth 1974, 1977, 1979
Mahony, Seamus 1979
Mailler, Patrick 1999
Maizel, Yefim 1994
Malagù, Stefania 1964, 1965, 1966
Malas, Spiro 1989
Malta, Alexander 1992
Malta, Alvaro 1977, 1978, 1979
Maltman, Christopher 1996
Manani, Ulderico 1996
Maney, Carla 1995
Manga, Silvanna 1987
Manning, Jane 1976
Mansfield, Louise 1972
Mantovani, Dino 1963
Marc, Alessandra 1987
Marchi, Claudia 1999
Marenzi, Angelo 1981
Margita, Stefan 1991
Mariani, Lorenzo 1995
Mariategui, Suso 1973
Mars, Jacques 1970
Marsh, David 1998
Martin, Emma 2000
Martin, Vivian 1972
Martirossian, Tigran 1998
Maruyama, Emiko 1976
Mason, Patrick 1987, 1988, 1989
Mátl, Lubomir 1995, 1996, 1997, 1998, 1999, 2000, 2001
Mátlová, Tereza 1997, 1999, 2000
Matorin, Vladimir 1993, 1995
Maunder, Dennis 1966
Maxwell, Donald 1981
Mazzola, Enrique 1997
Mc Guigan, Patrick 1966
McBrien, Peter 1984
McCafferty, Frances 1995

McCaffery, Michael 1986, 2001
McCaffrey, Patricia 1992
McCarney, Kate 1987, 1992
McCarry, Patricia 1963
McCosh, James 1974, 1975, 1976, 1977
McCoshan, Daniel 1954, 1955
McDonald, William 1973
McDonnell, Tom 1983
McGahon, Colette 1979
McGibbon, Roisin 1986
McGowan, Julian 2001
McGrenera, Seamus 1987
McGuigan, Patrick 1965
McKee, Richard 1973, 1974
McKenna, Eanna 2001
McKinney, Thomas 1974
McKinney, William 1974
McKinnon, Neil 1979
McMurray, John 1984
McNally, Brendan 1963
McVeigh, Tom 1993
McWilliams, Robin 1970
Meagher, Alison 1978, 1980
Medcalf, Stephen 1992, 1995
Mekler, Mani 1978, 1979
Melrose, Leigh 1998
Irish Ballet Irish Ballet Company 1977
Wexford Festival Chorus 1985
Mercer, Alexandra 1984
Merrigan, Joan 1982
Merry, Martin 1984
Mescheriakova, Marina 1994, 1995
Messana, John Angelo 1980
Michalopoulos, Eftimios 1969
Mihalik, Ales 2000
Mikelson, Keith 1990
Mikhailov, Maxim 1995, 1997, 1998
Miller, Katherine 1979
Miller, Kevin 1955
Miller, Lajos 1976, 1979
Miller, Ruth 1976, 1977
Mills, Mary 1993
Mitten, Seán 1974, 1976, 1980, 1981
Mixova, Ivana 1965

153

Monici, Gabriele 1993
Monogarova, Tatiana 2001
Montarsolo, Paolo 1957
Montgomery, Giovanna 1998
Montgomery, Kenneth 1964, 1970, 1971, 1972, 1973
Monti, Nicola 1952, 1953, 1954, 1956, 1959, 1962
Montresor, Beni 1995
Mooney, Kim 1980
Moores, Michael 1961
Moreno, Myrna 1971
Moretti, Amadeo 1996
Morgan Daymond, Karl 1992
Mori, Angelo 1966
Moriarty, Joan Denise 1951, 1977
Morozov, Igor 2000
Morozova, Ekaterina 2001
Morrell, Alan 1966
Morris, Bernie 1976, 1977
Morse, Anthony 1987
Mosley, George 1989
Mostart, Guus 1982, 1985
Moulton, Herbert 1964
Moyle, Julian 1959
Munk Rasmussen, Agnete 1996
Munteanu, Petre 1957
Munzer, Bettina 1988, 1989
Murchison, Ruari 1990, 1991
Murphy, Celine 1955
Murphy, Fiona 2000
Murphy, Patrick 1969, 1970, 1971, 1974, 1975, 1976, 1977
Murphy, Peter 1972
Murray, Ann 1974, 1975
Murray, Niamh 1994
Murray, Patrick 1967
Murray, Rupert 2000
Muzzi, Lonrenzo 1997
Myers, Pamela 1985

Nadler, Sheila 1989
Nakamaru, Michie 1995
National Philharmonic Orchestra of Belarus 2001

National Symphony Orchestra of Ireland 1990, 1991, 1992, 1993, 1994, 1995, 1996, 1997, 1998, 1999, 2000
Neilsen, Inga 1986
Newlands, Alastair 1964
Nezny, Igor 1997
Nicholson, Nigel 1982
Nickler, Reto 1994
Nicoletti, Mauro 1999
Nicoll, Harry 1974, 1981, 1982
Nicolov, Nicola 1959
Noble, Morag 1961
Noble, Noel 1964
Nolan, Brendan 1951
Nordin, Birgit 1965
Nordin, Lena 1988, 1989
Normand, Antoine 1990, 1993
Notare, Karen 1990, 1992
Novis, Constance 1990
Nowacki, Piotr 1999

O'Brien, Frank 1994
O'Brien, Greville 1978
O'Byrne, Carmel 1970
O'Byrne, Jurgen 1992
O'Connor, Angela 1951
O'Connor, Francis 1995
O'Connor, Gerard 1993
Oestman, Arnold 1986
O'Flynn, John 1983, 1985, 1986
Ognev, Vladimir 1996
O'Hara, Dermot 1951, 1952
O'Keeffe, Patricia 1952
O'Leary, Nora 1954, 1955, 1956, 1957, 1958, 1959, 1961, 1962, 1963, 1964, 1965, 1966
O'Leary, Peter 1976, 1978, 1979
Olegario, Frank 1964
Oliver, Alexander 1970, 1971
Ollmann, Kurt 1991
O'Neill, Dennis 1973, 1978
O'Neill, James 1975
Opie, Alan 1970, 1976
O'Reilly, Fiona 2000
O'Reirdan, Marie-Claire 1979, 1990
Ormerod, Nick 1985
Orolinova, Olga 1988

O'Rourke, Padraig 1980
O'Sullivan, Cara 1991
Otto, John 1982, 1985
Owens, Anne-Marie 1988

Page, Andrew 1972
Pagliuca, Silvano 1967, 1968, 1969
Pagoulatos, Panaghis 1990
Palazzi, Mirco 2001
Palla, Fabrizio 2000
Palmer, Felicity 1978
Panagulias, Ann 1991
Panajia, Sergio 1995
Pancek, Mark 1990
Panova, Mariana 2001
Panzavolta, Alessandra 1997
Parcher, William 1991, 1992
Parfitt, Wyndham 1966
Park, Jungwon 1994
Parker, David 1982
Parsons, Brian 1989
Pashley, Anne 1967, 1971, 1975
Passmore, William 1986
Patrick, Carmel 1978
Pazos, Angel 2001
Pearce, Colman 1981
Pedaci, Francesca 1995
Pedani, Paolo 1956, 1957, 1958, 1959, 1962
Pedrotti, Mark 1993
Peel, William 1993
Pelletier, Claude-Robin 1990
Pelliciari, Paolo 1997
Pendatchanska, Alexandrina 1996
Penkova, Reni 1973
Pentcheva, Mariana 1995
Perisson, Jean 1975
Peters, Johanna 1961, 1970, 1973
Peterson, Ingus 1987
Petroni, Luigi 1997
Pidò, Evelino 1991
Pierce, Dara 2000
Pike, Julian 1985
Pilou, Jeannette 1965
Pimlott, Stephen 1982, 1983
Piunti, Giuseppina 1996, 1997, 1998, 2001
Pivovarov, Valentin 2001
Plette, Marie 1994
Pleydell, Deirdre 1964, 1965
Poka, Balazs 1988
Polastri, Roberto 1996
Poli, Afro 1953
Pollard, Emma 1994

Pollock, Adam 1972, 1973, 1976
Popov, Valerij 1999
Potter, Peter 1956, 1958, 1959
Pountney, David 1972, 1973, 1978
Power, Patrick 1984
Praganza, Nelie 1968
Preece, Simon 1992
Priday, Huw 1991
Primrose, Claire 1987
Pring, Sarah 1992
Prior, Beniamino 1971
Pritchard, John 1959
Pritchard, Mark 1990
Pröbstl, Max 1955
Protti, Aldo 1959
Prügl, Radek 1998
Pugh, William 1979
Puglisi, Lino 1961, 1962, 1963, 1964
Puma, Salvatore 1955
Punt, Dacre 1974, 1977
Putkonen, Marko 1988
Pyant, Paul 1988

Radio Éireann Light Orchestra 1951, 1952, 1953, 1954, 1955, 1956, 1957, 1958, 1959
Radio Éireann Symphony Orchestra 1962, 1963, 1964, 1965
Radio Éireann Symphony Orchestra Players 1965
Radio Telefís Éireann Symphony Orchestra 1966, 1967, 1968, 1969, 1970, 1971, 1972, 1973, 1974, 1975, 1976, 1977, 1978, 1979, 1980, 1981, 1982, 1983, 1984, 1985, 1986, 1987, 1988, 1989
Rae, William 1989
Ramella, Elvina 1952, 1953
Ransome, Antony 1974
Raponi, Vincenzo 1997, 1998, 1999
Rath, John 1992
Ratti, Eugenia 1969
Rayam, Curtis 1976, 1980, 1981, 1986
Read, John B 1977

Reakes, Patricia 1970
Reddin, Jeanie 1963
Redmon, Robynne 1987
Reece, Arley 1973, 1974
Reed, Tim 1977, 1978, 1979, 1980, 1981, 1983, 1987
Reid, Alex 1974, 1977
Reid, Ian 1985, 1986
Reiffenstuel, Brigitte 1996
Reinhardt-Kiss, Ursula 1982
Reiter-Soffer, Domy 1977
Réthy, Esther 1955
Reynolds, Anna 1963, 1966
Reynolds, Kenneth 1967
Rhys-Evans, Huw 1991
Ricchelli, Giorgio 1999, 2001
Rice, Peter 1955
Richard, Lawerence 1990
Richardson, Hugh 1972
Rigacci, Bruno 1990
Rigacci, Susanna 1984
Rinaldi, Margherita 1963
Rinaldi-Miliani, Stefano 1997
Ring, Patricia 1970
Ring, Patrick 1972
Rinn, Inka 1999
Ripa di Meana, Franco 1997
Ristori, Gabrielle 1970
Robertson, Toby 1984
Robinson, Peter 197272
Robson, Richard 1982, 1984, 1985, 1994, 1995, 1996
Roche, Seamus 1951
Rose, Gregory 1993, 1994
Rosen, Albert 1965, 1966, 1967, 1972, 1973, 1974, 1976, 1978
Rosen, Albert 1982, 1983, 1984, 1985, 1986, 1987, 1988, 1989, 1992, 1994
Rossi, Elena 1997
Rota, Marcello 2000
Rothmüller, Marko 1955, 1956
Rouleau, Joseph 1973, 1978
Roy, Alexander 1968
Royal Liverpool Philharmonic Orchestra 1961
Rozario, Patricia 1989

Rumstadt, Guido Johannes 1992
Runge, Peter-Christophe 1984, 1990, 1991
Rust, Elizabeth 1961

Sacher, Jürgen 1992
Safina, Alessandro 1997
Saks, Gidon 1994
Saldari, Luciano 1962
Salminen, Matti 1973
Salomaa, Petteri 1985, 1986
Salsi, Luca 2001
Samar, Pari 1968
Sanchi, Edoardo 1997
Sand, Malmfrid 1983, 1988
Sandison, Gordon 1981, 1983, 1990
Sandor, John 1975
Sandvé, Kjell Magnus 1993
Saque, Zuelika 1967
Sarti, Laura 1961, 1962, 1964
Sauramo, Marit 1991, 1994
Schnitzler, Claude 1999
Schwengl, Bruno 1993, 1994
Sciutti, Graziella 1957
Scott, Michael 1974
Selesnev, Georgi 1992
Sendor, Jan 1977
Serkin, Valery 1994
Serville, Roberto 1996
Seymour, Di 1986
Shacklock, Contance 1956
Shanahan, Mark 1992
Sharkey, Nicola 1981
Sharp, Rebecca 2001
Sharpe, Ivan 1994
Sharpe, Terence 1967, 1969, 1979, 1980
Sharples, Harold 1971
Sheil, Fergus 1995
Shelley, Grant 1983, 1984
Sheridan, Mary 1972
Sheridan, Pat 1978, 1979
Sherlock, Ceri 1990
Sherratt, Brindley 1986
Shopland, Martin 1979
Sieden, Cyndia 1989
Sinclair, Monica 1955
Siukola, Heikki 1972
Skoglund, Annika 1990
Slack, Adrian 1974, 1975, 1976, 1978

Sleep, Kevin 1989
Šlepkovská, Denisa 1996
Slorach, Marie 1981, 1984
Smith, Jennifer 1977
Smith, Kevin 1977
Socci, Gianni 1978, 1979, 1981, 1983
Soldh, Anita 1989
Sorbello, Giuseppe 1965
Soumagnas, Juan 1971, 1975
Soyer, Roger 1968
Sparvoli, Fabio 1999, 2001
Speight, Christopher 1989
Spencer, Theodore 1985
Spencer Williams, Simon 1994
Spina, Mario 1957
Springer, Maureen 1951
Stachura, Dariusz 1999
Staern, Gunnar 1962, 1963, 1964, 1965
Stapleton, Robin 1980, 1982
Steger, Ingrid 1983
Steinberg, Paul 1994
Steinberg, Pinchas 1979
Stephen, Pamela Helen 1990
Stephinger, Christoph 1989
Stevens, Roy 1995
Stewart, John 1970, 1971
Stilgoe, Richard 1973
Stockhaus, Björn 1989
Stoddart, John 1967, 1968, 1971
Stone, William 1989
Strasfogel, Ian 1975
Straw, Hilary 1977
Stubbs, Annena 1983
Sutcliff, Richard 1985
Sutcliffe, Jeremy 1974, 1976
Svensson, Peter 1994
Swensen, Robert 1994
Świdzinski, Leszek 1999
Symonds, Clair 1977

Tadeo, Giorgio 1959
Tagger, Nicola 1967
Takova, Darina 1996
Talbot, Oenone 1970
Talfryn, Philip 1958
Tarassov, Igor 2000
Tarrés, Enriqueta 1963
Tatlow, Caroline 1978
Taylor, Jamie 1974

Teliga, Aleksander 2000
Terzian, Anita 1982
Testa, Arturo 1984
The Young Wexford Singers 2001
Thompson, Adrian 1985
Thompson, Martin 1989
Tingaud, Jean-Luc 2001
Tinsley, Pauline 1986, 1990
Tonini, Antonio 1962
Torday, Robert 1992
Torella, Alessandra 1999, 2001
Tortelier, Yan Pascal 1983, 1984, 1986
Tosi, Giancarlo 1987, 1994
Tovey, Julian 1998
Trakas, Christopher 1992
Trama, Ugo 1961
Traxel, Josef 1956
Trebeleva, Katia 1997, 2000
Trew, Graham 1978
Trotter, Stewart 1979, 1980
Tsymbala, Roman 1993
Tudor, Stephen 1969
Tulubieva, Tatyana 1997
Tynan, Kathleen 1986, 1987, 1988, 1989
Tyrrel, Timothy 1981

Uecker, Korliss 1992
Ulfung, Ragnar 1961
Ulivieri, Nicola 1997

Vacis, Gabriele 1998
Vajnar, Frantisek 1989
Valentini, Alberta 1964, 1966
Vallat, Michel 1975
van Allan, Richard 1967, 1968
van Bork, Hanneke 1968
Vaněk, Joe 1987, 1988, 1989
Vanelli, Gino 1952
Vanzo, Alain 1961
Vassileva, Svetelina 1996
Vavrille, Annie 1997
Veda, Elmira 1998
Veira, Jonathan 1986, 1994
Velazco, Eduardo 1971
Venables, Jane 1972
Ventre, Carlo 1995

Ventriglia, Franco 1961, 1962, 1963, 1964
Vick, Graham 1981
Videnov, Ljubomir 1985
Vietheer, Erich 1965
Vincenzi, Simon 1993
Vinklarek, Jiři 1998
Visser, Lieuwe 1974
Vivarelli, Gisela 1956
Vizin, Viktoria 1998, 1999
Vizioli, Stefano 1996
Voldrich, Milan 1988
Volonté, Dario 1998, 1999
Voloschuk, Alexandre 1997, 2001
von Dohnanyi, Oliver 1991
von Duisburg, Johannes 1992
Von Kannen, Gunter 1982

Wagner, Wolf Siegfried 1974, 1977
Wakefield, John 1968
Walker, Lyn 1970
Walker, Malcolm 1991
Waller, Michael 1968
Wallis, Delia 1968, 1970, 1972
Walsh, Donal 1988
Walsh, Evelyn 1988
Walsh, Louise 1998
Walsh, Nellie 1951, 1972, 1991
Walsh I.B.V.M., Sr Mary 1976, 1977, 1979
Walton, Gavin 1971
Ward, Henry 1969
Waterhouse, John 1986, 1987
Watson, Curtis 1986
Watson, Lillian 1970
Watt, Alan 1978
Way, Laura 1990
Webb, Jonathan 1989, 1990, 1991
Webster, Jane 1987
Wedd, Peter 1998
Weinorowski, Wjacheslav 1993, 1994, 1995
Weiss, Isadora 1999
Werba, Markus 2001
Wexford Childrens Chorus 1977, 1979, 1986, 1997
Wexford Festival Baroque Ensemble 1975

Wexford Festival Chorus 1951, 1952, 1953, 1954, 1955, 1956, 1957, 1958, 1959, 1961, 1962, 1963, 1964, 1965, 1966, 1967, 1968, 1969, 1970, 1971, 1972, 1973, 1974, 1975, 1976, 1977, 1978, 1979, 1980, 1981, 1982, 1983, 1984, 1985, 1986, 1987, 1988, 1989, 1990, 1991, 1992, 1993, 1994, 1995, 1996, 1997, 1998, 1999, 2000, 2001
Wexford Festival Ensemble 1976
Wexford Festival Male Chorus 1986
Wexford School of Ballet & Modern Dance 1989, 1990, 1991
White, Robert 1978
Whittingham, Angela 1970
Wicks, Dennis 1959, 1961
Wilborn, Kip 1992
Wilding, Simon 1998
Williams, Bradley 1993
Williams, Janet 1991
Williams, Malcolm 1970
Willis, Nuala 1981, 1984, 1985
Wilson, Catherine 1976
Wilson, Christine 1965
Wilson, Dorothy 1963
Winberg, Annalisa 1995
Winfield, John 1980
Winkler, Jutta 1992, 1993
Winston, Lee 1976
Wittges, Max 1990, 1999
Won Lee, Jeong 1998
Wong, Julie 1988
Woodhouse, Kim-Marie 1996
Woods, Elizabeth 1999
Woollett, Elizabeth 1991
Woolley, Reginald 1961, 1962, 1963, 1964, 1965, 1966
Wright, Chloë 1999
Wright, Finbar 1988
Wright, Patricia 1987
Wroblewski, Patryk 1994

Yao Yu, Guo 1992
Yinon, Israel 1998
York Skinner, John 1975

Young, Alexander 1969

Zahradníček, František 1998, 1999, 2000, 2001
Zambello, Francesca 1988, 1989, 1991, 1993
Zanini, Nicoletta 1995
Zannoth, Sherry 1985
Zelenskaia, Elena 1999
Zeller, Richard 1992
Zelnickova, Roberta 1999
Zidek, Ivo 1972
Zimnenko, Leonid 1994
Znaniecki, Michal 1999
Zulian, Renzo 2000
Zwierko, Agnieszka 2000

Officers
1951 – 2001

President
1951-1972
Sir Compton MacKenzie
1974-1976
Lauder Greenway
1977-1992
Sir Alfred Beit
1993-
Sir Anthony O'Reilly

Chairman
1951-1955
Tom Walsh
1956-1961
Fr. M. J. O'Neill
1962-1966
Sir Alfred Beit
1967-1970
Dr. J. D. Ffrench
1971-1976
Seán Scallan
1977-1979
Brig. Richard Jefferies
1980-1985
Jim Golden
1986-1991
Barbara Wallace
1992-1997
John O'Connor
1998-
Ted Howlin

Artistic Director
1951-1966
Tom Walsh
1967-1973
Brian Dickie
1974-1978
Thomson Smillie
1979-1981
Adrian Slack
1982-1994
Elaine Padmore
1995-
Luigi Ferrari

Chief Executive
1988-
Jerome Hynes